WINTER
BLOOMS

TWENTY ONE DESIGNS
BY KIM HARGREAVES

CREDITS

DESIGNS & STYLING — Kim Hargreaves

PHOTOGRAPHY & EDITORIAL DESIGN — Graham Watts

EDITOR — Kathleen Hargreaves

HAIR & MAKE-UP — Diana Fisher

MODELS — Angharad Hunt, Fiona Beck, Hannah Wright, Rebecca Hodgson & Rufus

LAYOUTS — Angela Lin

PATTERNS — Sue Whiting & Trisha McKenzie

© Copyright Kim Hargreaves 2009

Published in 2009 by Kim Hargreaves

Intake Cottage, 26 Underbank Old Road, Holmfirth

West Yorkshire, HD9 1EA, England

British Library Cataloguing in Publication Data

A catalogue record for this book is available from the British Library

ISBN-10   1—906487—06—5

ISBN-13 978—1—906487—06—5

CONTENTS

THE DESIGNS

At a secluded country castle the drama unfolds...
Delicate mohair, lightweight cashmere & classic tweeds
are adorned by dipping into winter's dressing up box to
joyful delight. Discover a treasure trove of eccentric style.

Delectably delightful...
This page,
Angharad wears
DELPHINE, a sculpted
peplum jacket.
Opposite, Rebecca is
wearing DIVINE a
cabled shrug.

9

Celebrating the
seasons rich tones...
This page, Hannah
wears SAFFRON &
OPAL wrap.
Opposite Fiona
wears BRIAR
sweater dress.

10

Holme
Castle

Please Press
and
Enter

This is a
no - smoking
establishment

The picture of elegance...
This page, Rebecca is
wearing ALEXI, an
utterly classic cardigan.
Opposite CHERRY a
pretty beret.

Oh so chic...
This page, Angharad
is wearing CHERRY a
classic beret. Opposite
Rebecca in ALEXI.

15

*True glamour...
This page, Fiona
wears DIVINE a
cabled shrug, whilst
Hannah opposite
looks ravishing in
RYDER sweater.*

Dramatically demure...
This page, Rebecca
wears OPAL wrap.
Opposite, Hannah is
wearing RYDER
a cabled sweater.

19

A true bloom...
This page, Angharad
wears EVE, a frothy
stripy scarf & opposite
CHAISE, the most
classic of sweaters.

Tally-ho!
Hannah in a most
mischievous mood,
wears REBECCA
a neat fitted jacket.

25

Very Coco…
Angharad looks most
glamorous in RAVEN,
a chic tailored jacket
with antique buttons.

Bowled over...
Angharad looks
stunning wearing
SORREL a tweed
A-line jacket.

Oh so pretty in pink...
Hannah is wearing
MERRY, a very
Sloppy Joe !

A touch of the orient... This page, Angharad looks truly beautiful in OPAL, while opposite Fiona is luscious in LIVI.

Full of froth & flounce...
Hannah is fabulous in
EMERALD, a beaded
trimmed sweater.

Fiona strikes a pose in INDIGO, a stylish duster coat adorned with antique buttons.

40

*Natty in navy...
Opposite Hannah
wears FLEUR a
neat sweater with
lace ruffle trim.*

42

*Blown away...
This page, Angharad
wears BRIAR sweater.
Opposite, Hannah is
wearing TEAL, a very
versatile cardigan.*

Abracadabra!!!
Fiona showcases
VALENTINE, a
neat collared cape.

Holme
Castle

Please Press
and
Enter

This is a
no - smoking
establishment

Pure sophistication in diamante & pearls, Rebecca wears TEAL, a drapey cardigan, whilst Rufus stands guard.

*Deliciously decadent...
This page Fiona
is wearing CHERRY
beret. Opposite,
Angharad wears
GARNET cardigan
& Hannah wears
EMERALD.*

51

THE
PATTERNS

Recommendation

Suitable for the knitter with a little experience
Please see pages 6 & 10 for photographs.

	XS	S	M	L	XL	XXL	
To fit	**81**	**86**	**91**	**97**	**102**	**109**	**cm**
bust	32	34	36	38	40	43	in

Rowan Lima

9	9	10	10	11	12	x 50gm

Photographed in Puno

Needles

1 pair 5mm (no 6) (US 8) needles
1 pair 5½mm (no 5) (US 9) needles

Buttons · 7

Tension

20 sts and 25 rows to 10 cm measured over
stocking stitch using 5½mm (US 9) needles.

BACK

Cast on 210 (222: 240: 252: 270: 294) sts
using 5½mm (US 9) needles.
Row 1 (RS): *K1, P1, rep from * to end.
Row 2: *P1, K1, rep from * to end.
Rows 3 and 4: As rows 1 and 2.
Beg with a K row, work in st st as folls:
Work 2 rows, ending with a WS row.
Row 7 (RS): *K4, K2tog, rep from * to end.
175 (185: 200: 210: 225: 245) sts.
Work 5 rows.
Row 13: *K3, K2tog, rep from * to end.
140 (148: 160: 168: 180: 196) sts.
Work 3 rows.
Row 17: *K2, K2tog, rep from * to end.
105 (111: 120: 126: 135: 147) sts.
Work 2 rows.
Row 20 (WS): *P2tog, P1, rep from * to end.
70 (74: 80: 84: 90: 98) sts.
These 20 rows complete peplum frill.
Place markers at both ends of last row.
Work 6 rows, ending with a WS row.
Next row (dec) (RS): K3, K2tog, K to last
5 sts, K2tog tbl, K3.
68 (72: 78: 82: 88: 96) sts.
Work 17 rows, ending with a WS row.
Next row (inc) (RS): K3, M1, K to last 3 sts,
M1, K3.**
Working all side seam increases as set by last
row, inc 1 st at each end of 8th and 5 foll 6th
rows. 82 (86: 92: 96: 102: 110) sts.
Cont straight until back measures 28 (28: 29:
29: 29: 29) cm **from markers**, ending with a
WS row.
Shape armholes
Cast off 3 (4: 4: 5: 5: 6) sts at beg of next
2 rows. 76 (78: 84: 86: 92: 98) sts.
Dec 1 st at each end of next 3 (3: 5: 5: 7: 9)
rows, then on foll 3 (3: 3: 3: 3: 2) alt rows,
then on foll 4th row.
62 (64: 66: 68: 70: 74) sts.
Cont straight until armhole measures 18 (19:
19: 20: 21: 22) cm, ending with a WS row.
Shape shoulders and back neck
Cast off 5 (5: 6: 6: 6: 7) sts at beg of next
2 rows. 52 (54: 54: 56: 58: 60) sts.
Next row (RS): Cast off 5 (5: 6: 6: 6: 7) sts,
K until there are 10 (10: 9: 9: 10: 10) sts
on right needle and turn, leaving rem sts
on a holder.

Work each side of neck separately.
Cast off 4 sts at beg of next row.
Cast off rem 6 (6: 5: 5: 6: 6) sts.
With RS facing, rejoin yarn to rem sts, cast off
centre 22 (24: 24: 26: 26: 26) sts, K to end.
Complete to match first side, reversing
shapings.

FRONT

Work as given for back to **.
Working all side seam increases as set by last
row, cont as folls:
Work 3 rows, ending with a WS row.
Divide for front opening
Next row (RS): K32 (34: 37: 39: 42: 46) and
turn, leaving rem sts on a holder.
Work each side separately.
Next row (WS): Cast on and K 6 sts, P to end.
38 (40: 43: 45: 48: 52) sts.
Next row: Knit.
Next row: Purl.
Next row: K3, M1, K to last 6 sts, P6.
Next row: K6, P to end.
Last 4 rows set the sts – front opening edge 6
sts in ridge patt with all other sts still in st st.
Cont as set, inc 1 st at beg of 5th and 4 foll
6th rows. 44 (46: 49: 51: 54: 58) sts.
Cont straight until front matches back to beg
of armhole shaping, ending with a WS row.
Shape armhole
Keeping sts correct, cast off 3 (4: 4: 5: 5: 6)
sts at beg of next row.
41 (42: 45: 46: 49: 52) sts.
Work 1 row.
Dec 1 st at armhole edge of next 3 (3: 5: 5: 7:
9) rows, then on foll 3 (3: 3: 3: 3: 2) alt rows,
then on foll 4th row.
34 (35: 36: 37: 38: 40) sts.
Cont straight until 16 (16: 16: 18: 18: 18)
rows less have been worked than on back to
beg of shoulder shaping, ending with a WS
row.
Shape neck
Next row (RS): K23 (23: 24: 25: 26: 28) and
turn, leaving rem 11 (12: 12: 12: 12: 12) sts
on another holder.
Dec 1 st at neck edge of next 4 rows, then on
foll 2 (2: 2: 3: 3: 3) alt rows, then on foll 4th
row. 16 (16: 17: 17: 18: 20) sts.
Work 3 rows, ending with a WS row.

Shape shoulder

Cast off 5 (5: 6: 6: 6: 7) sts at beg of next and foll alt row.

Work 1 row.

Cast off rem 6 (6: 5: 5: 6: 6) sts.

Mark positions for 7 buttons along left front opening edge – first button level with 5th row up from base of front opening, top button to come just above neck shaping, and rem 5 buttons evenly spaced between.

With RS facing, rejoin yarn to rem sts and cont as folls:

Next row (RS): P6, K to end.

38 (40: 43: 45: 48: 52) sts.

Next row: P to last 6 sts, K6.

Next row: Knit.

Next row: Purl.

Last 4 rows set the sts – front opening edge 6 sts in ridge patt with all other sts still in st st.

Next row (WS): Patt 2 sts, work 2 tog, yrn (to make a buttonhole), patt to last 3 sts, M1, K3.

Making a further 5 buttonholes in this way to correspond with positions marked for buttons along left front opening edge, complete to match first side, reversing shapings and working first row of neck shaping as folls:

Shape neck

Next row (RS): Patt 11 (12: 12: 12: 12: 12) sts and slip these sts onto another holder, K to end.

23 (23: 24: 25: 26: 28) sts.

SLEEVES (both alike)

Cast on 38 (40: 40: 42: 44: 46) sts using 5mm (US 8) needles.

Row 1 (RS): K0 (0: 0: 0: 1: 0), P0 (1: 1: 2: 2: 0), *K2, P2, rep from * to last 2 (3: 3: 0: 1: 2) sts, K2 (2: 2: 0: 1: 2), P0 (1: 1: 0: 0: 0).

Row 2: P0 (0: 0: 0: 1: 0), K0 (1: 1: 2: 2: 0), *P2, K2, rep from * to last 2 (3: 3: 0: 1: 2) sts, P2 (2: 2: 0: 1: 2), K0 (1: 1: 0: 0: 0).

These 2 rows form rib.

Work in rib for a further 16 rows, inc 1 st at each end of 15th of these rows and ending with a WS row. 40 (42: 42: 44: 46: 48) sts.

Change to 5½mm (US 9) needles.

Beg with a K row and working all sleeve increases in same way as side seam increases, now work in st st, shaping sides by inc 1 st at each end of 7th and every foll 8th row to 44 (52: 50: 60: 60: 68) sts, then on every foll 10th row until there are 58 (62: 62: 66: 68: 72) sts.

Cont straight until sleeve measures 46 (47: 48: 49: 50: 51) cm, ending with a WS row.

Shape top

Cast off 3 (4: 4: 5: 5: 6) sts at beg of next 2 rows.

52 (54: 54: 56: 58: 60) sts.

Dec 1 st at each end of next 3 rows, then on foll alt row, then on 5 foll 4th rows. 34 (36: 36: 38: 40: 42) sts.

Work 1 row.

Dec 1 st at each end of next and every foll alt row to 30 sts, then on foll 3 rows, ending with a WS row.

Cast off rem 24 sts.

MAKING UP

Pin the pieces out and steam gently without allowing the iron to touch the yarn.

Join both shoulder seams using back stitch or mattress stitch if preferred.

Neckband

With RS facing and using 5mm (US 8) needles, slip 11 (12: 12: 12: 12: 12) sts from right front holder onto right needle, rejoin yarn and pick up and knit 18 (18: 18: 20: 20: 20) sts up right side of neck, 30 (32: 32: 34: 34: 34) sts from back, and 18 (18: 18: 20: 20: 20) sts down left side of neck, then patt across 11 (12: 12: 12: 12: 12) sts on left front holder.

88 (92: 92: 98: 98: 98) sts.

Work in rev st st for 4 rows, making 7th buttonhole on 2nd of these rows and ending a **RS** row.

Cast off knitwise (on **WS**).

Join side seams.

Join sleeve seams.

Insert sleeves into armholes.

At base of front opening, sew left front cast-on edge in place on inside.

Sew on buttons.

54 (55: 56: 57: 58: 59) cm
21¼ (21½: 22: 22½: 23: 23¼) in

41 (43: 46: 48: 51: 55) cm
16 (17: 18: 19: 20: 21½) in

46 (47: 48: 49: 50: 51) cm
18 (18½: 19: 19¼: 19¾: 20) in

Recommendation

Suitable for the knitter with a little experience
Please see pages 11 & 44 for photographs.

	XS	S	M	L	XL	XXL	
To fit	**81**	**86**	**91**	**97**	**102**	**109**	**cm**
bust	32	34	36	38	40	43	in

Rowan Lima

| **Dress** | 11 | 12 | 13 | 14 | 15 | 16 | x 50gm |
| **Sweter** | 8 | 9 | 10 | 11 | 12 | 13 | x 50gm |

Dress photographed in Pampas, & sweater in
Amazon

Needles

1 pair 4½mm (no 7) (US 7) needles
1 pair 5mm (no 6) (US 8) needles
1 pair 5½mm (no 5) (US 9) needles

Tension

20 sts and 25 rows to 10 cm measured over
stocking stitch using 5½mm (US 9) needles.

BRIAR
DRESS & SWEATER WITH GENEROUS NECKLINE

DRESS
BACK
Cast on 90 (94: 98: 102: 110: 118) sts using
5mm (US 8) needles.
Row 1 (RS): K2, *P2, K2, rep from * to end.
Row 2: P2, *K2, P2, rep from * to end.
These 2 rows form rib.
Cont in rib for a further 30 rows, dec 1 (1: 0:
0: 1: 1) st at each end of last row and ending
with a WS row.
88 (92: 98: 102: 108: 116) sts.
Change to 5½mm (US 9) needles.
Beg with a K row, cont in st st as folls:
Work straight until back measures 24 cm,
ending with a WS row.
Next row (dec) (RS): K3, K2tog, K to last
5 sts, K2tog tbl, K3.
Working all side seam decreases as
set by last row, dec 1 st at each end
of 10th and 2 foll 8th rows, then on
4 foll 6th rows.
72 (76: 82: 86: 92: 100) sts.
Cont straight until back measures 52 cm,
ending with a WS row.
Next row (inc) (RS): K3, M1, K to last 3 sts,
M1, K3.
Working all size seam increases as set by
last row, inc 1 st at each end of 10th and
3 foll 10th rows.
82 (86: 92: 96: 102: 110) sts.
Cont straight until back measures
72 (72: 73: 73: 73: 73) cm, ending
with a WS row.
Shape raglan armholes
Cast off 5 sts at beg of next 2 rows.
72 (76: 82: 86: 92: 100) sts.
Work 2 (2: 2: 2: 2: 0) rows.
Sizes XS, S, M and L only
Next row (RS): K1, K2tog, K to last 3 sts,
K2tog tbl, K1.
Work 3 rows.
Rep last 4 rows 4 (4: 1: 1: -: -) times more.
62 (66: 78: 82: -: -) sts.
Size XXL only
Next row (RS): K1, K2tog, K to last 3 sts,
K2tog tbl, K1.
Next row: P1, P2tog tbl, P to last 3 sts,
P2tog, P1.
Rep last 2 rows once more.
92 sts.

All sizes
Next row (RS): K1, K2tog, K to last 3 sts,
K2tog tbl, K1.
Work 1 row.
Rep last 2 rows 2 (3: 9: 10: 15: 15) times
more, ending with a WS row.
56 (58: 58: 60: 60: 60) sts.
Shape back neck
Next row (RS): K1, K2tog, K3 and turn,
leaving rem sts on a holder. 5 sts.
Work each side of neck separately.
Next row (WS): P2tog, P3.
Next row: K1, K3tog.
Next row: P2tog and fasten off.
With RS facing, rejoin yarn to rem sts, cast
off centre 44 (46: 46: 48: 48: 48) sts,
K to last 3 sts, K2tog tbl, K1. 5 sts.
Next row (WS): P3, P2tog.
Next row: Sl 1, K2tog, psso, K1.
Next row: P2tog and fasten off.

FRONT
Work as given for back until 64 (66: 68: 70:
70: 70) sts rem in raglan armhole shaping.
Work 3 (1: 1: 1: 1: 1) rows, ending with
a WS row.
Shape front neck
Next row (RS): (K1, K2tog) 1 (0: 1: 1: 1: 1)
times, K11 (14: 12: 12: 12: 12) and turn,
leaving rem sts on a holder.
13 (14: 14: 14: 14: 14) sts.
Work each side of neck separately.
Dec 1 st at neck edge of next 7 rows, ending
with a WS row, **and at same time** dec 1 st at
raglan armhole edge of 4th (2nd: 2nd: 2nd:
2nd: 2nd) and foll 1 (2: 2: 2: 2: 2) alt rows.
4 sts.
Next row (RS): K1, K3tog.
Next row: P2tog and fasten off.
With RS facing, rejoin yarn to rem sts, cast
off centre 36 (38: 38: 40: 40: 40) sts, K to
last 3 (0: 3: 3: 3: 3) sts, (K2tog tbl, K1) 1 (0:
1: 1: 1: 1) times. 13 (14: 14: 14: 14: 14) sts.
Dec 1 st at neck edge of next 7 rows, ending
with a WS row, **and at same time** dec 1 st at
raglan armhole edge of 4th (2nd: 2nd: 2nd:
2nd: 2nd) and foll 1 (2: 2: 2: 2: 2) alt rows.
4 sts.
Next row: Sl 1, K2tog, psso, K1.
Next row: P2tog and fasten off.

SLEEVES (both alike)

Cast on 38 (40: 42: 44: 46: 48) sts using 5mm (US 8) needles.

Row 1 (RS): P0 (1: 0: 1: 0: 1), K2, *P2, K2, rep from * to last 0 (1: 0: 1: 0: 1) st, P0 (1: 0: 1: 0: 1).

Row 2: K0 (1: 0: 1: 0: 1), P2, *K2, P2, rep from * to last 0 (1: 0: 1: 0: 1) st, K0 (1: 0: 1: 0: 1).

These 2 rows form rib.

Cont in rib, inc 1 st at each end of 7th (7th: 9th: 9th: 9th: 9th) and 1 (0: 0: 0: 0: 0) foll 10th row, then on foll 12th row. 44 (44: 46: 48: 50: 52) sts.

Work a further 1 (11: 9: 9: 9: 9) rows, ending with a WS row.

Change to 5½mm (US 9) needles.

Beg with a K row and working all sleeve increases in same way as side seam increases, cont in st st, shaping sides by inc 1 st at each end of 11th (next: 3rd: 3rd: 3rd: 3rd) and every foll 12th row to 58 (60: 62: 62: 60: 60) sts, then on every foll - (-: -: 14th: 14th: 14th) row until there are - (-: -: 64: 66: 68) sts.

Cont straight until sleeve measures 51 (52: 53: 54: 55: 56) cm, ending with a WS row.

Shape raglan

Cast off 5 sts at beg of next 2 rows. 48 (50: 52: 54: 56: 58) sts.

Working all raglan decreases in same way as given for raglan armholes, dec 1 st at each end of 3rd and 6 foll 4th rows, then on foll 0 (0: 1: 2: 3: 4) alt rows. 34 (36: 36: 36: 36: 36) sts.

Work 1 (3: 1: 1: 1: 1) rows, ending with a WS row.

Left sleeve only

Cast off 11 (12: 12: 12: 12: 12) sts at beg and dec 0 (1: 1: 1: 1: 1) st at end of next row. 23 sts.

Work 1 row.

Cast off 11 sts at beg and dec 1 st at end of next row.

Work 1 row.

Right sleeve only

Dec 0 (1: 1: 1: 1: 1) st at each end of next row, then cast off 11 (12: 12: 12: 12: 12) sts at beg of foll row. 23 sts.

Dec 1 st at beg of next row, then cast off 11 sts at beg of foll row.

Both sleeves

Cast off rem 11 sts.

MAKING UP

Pin the pieces out and steam gently without allowing the iron to touch the yarn.

Join both front and right back raglan seams using back stitch or mattress stitch if preferred.

Neckband

With RS facing and using 5mm (US 9) needles, pick up and knit 31 sts from top of left sleeve, placing marker on centre st of these sts, pick up and knit 8 sts down left side of neck, 36 (38: 38: 40: 40: 40) sts from front, 8 sts up right side of neck, and 31 sts from top of right sleeve, placing marker on centre st of these sts, then pick up and knit 48 (50: 50: 52: 52: 52) sts from back. 162 (166: 166: 170: 170: 170) sts.

Rows 1 to 3: Knit.

Row 4 (RS): *K to within 5 sts of marked st, K3tog tbl, K5 (marked st is centre st of these 5 sts), K3tog, rep from * once more, K to end. 154 (158: 158: 162: 162: 162) sts.

Rows 5 to 8: As rows 1 to 4. 146 (150: 150: 154: 154: 154) sts.

Change to 4½mm (US 7) needles.

Rows 9 to 12: As rows 1 to 4. 138 (142: 142: 146: 146: 146) sts.

Cast off knitwise (on **WS**).

Join left back raglan and neckband seam. Join side and sleeve seams.

SWEATER

BACK

Cast on 86 (90: 94: 98: 106: 114) sts using 5mm (US 8) needles.

Row 1 (RS): K2, *P2, K2, rep from * to end.

Row 2: P2, *K2, P2, rep from * to end.

These 2 rows form rib.

Cont in rib for a further 14 rows, dec 1 (1: 0: 0: 1: 1) st at each end of last row and ending with a WS row. 84 (88: 94: 98: 104: 112) sts.

Change to 5½mm (US 9) needles.

Beg with a K row, cont in st st as folls:

Work 4 rows, ending with a WS row.

Next row (dec) (RS): K3, K2tog, K to last 5 sts, K2tog tbl, K3.

Working all side seam decreases as set by last row, dec 1 st at each end of 6th and 4 foll 6th rows. 72 (76: 82: 86: 92: 100) sts.

Cont straight until back measures 28 cm, ending with a WS row.

Next row (inc) (RS): K3, M1, K to last 3 sts, M1, K3.

Working all size seam increases as set by last row, inc 1 st at each end of 10th and 3 foll 10th rows. 82 (86: 92: 96: 102: 110) sts.

Cont straight until back measures 48 (48: 49: 49: 49: 49) cm, ending with a WS row.

Complete as given for back of dress from beg of raglan armhole shaping.

FRONT

Work as given for back until 64 (66: 68: 70: 70: 70) sts rem in raglan armhole shaping.

Work 3 (1: 1: 1: 1: 1) rows, ending with a WS row.

Complete as given for front of dress from beg of front neck shaping.

SLEEVES (both alike)

Work as given for sleeves of dress.

MAKING UP

Work as given for dress.

SWEATER

DRESS

69 [70: 71: 72: 73: 74] cm
27 [27½: 28: 28½: 28¾: 29] in

93 [94: 95: 96: 97: 98] cm
36½ [37: 37½: 37¾: 38¼: 38½] in

41 [43: 46: 48: 51: 55] cm
16 [17: 18: 19: 20: 21½] in

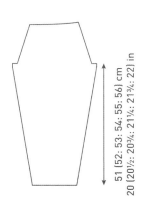

51 [52: 53: 54: 55: 56] cm
20 [20½: 20¾: 21¼: 21¾: 22] in

DELPHINE

AN ELEGANT TWEEDY PEPLUM JACKET

Recommendation

Suitable for the knitter with a little experience
Please see page 9 for photograph.

	XS	S	M	L	XL	XXL	
To fit	**81**	**86**	**91**	**97**	**102**	**109**	cm
bust	32	34	36	38	40	43	in

Rowan Felted Tweed

| 6 | 7 | 7 | 8 | 8 | 9 | x 50gm |

Photographed in Cinnamon

Needles

1 pair 3¼mm (no 10) (US 3) needles
1 pair 3¾mm (no 9) (US 5) needles
Cable needle

Buttons – 6 large & 6 small

Tension

25 sts and 34 rows to 10 cm measured over
double moss stitch using 3¾mm (US 5)
needles.

SPECIAL ABBREVIATIONS

C10B = slip next 5 sts onto cable needle and
leave at back of work, K5, then K5 from cable
needle; **C10F** = slip next 5 sts onto cable
needle and leave at front of work, K5, then
K5 from cable needle; **C14B** = slip next 7 sts
onto cable needle and leave at back of work,
K7, then K7 from cable needle; **C14F** = slip
next 7 sts onto cable needle and leave at front
of work, K7, then K7 from cable needle.

BACK

Cast on 145 (151: 157: 163: 169: 181) sts
using 3¾mm (US 5) needles.
Row 1 (RS): P1 (0: 1: 0: 1: 1), (K1, P1) 6 (8:
8: 10: 10: 13) times, (P9, inc once in each of
next 7 sts) twice, P9, K1, (P1, K1) 18 (18: 20:
20: 22: 22) times, wrap next st (by slipping
next st from left needle to right needle, taking
yarn to opposite side of work between needles
and then slipping same st back onto left
needle – when working back across wrapped
sts work the wrapped st and the wrapping
loop tog as one st) and turn.
Row 2: K1, (P1, K1) 18 (18: 20: 20: 22: 22)
times, wrap next st and turn.
Row 3: P1, (K1, P1) 18 (18: 20: 20: 22: 22)
times, P9, inc once in each of next 7 sts, wrap
next st and turn.
Row 4: P14, K9, P1, (K1, P1) 18 (18: 20:
20: 22: 22) times, K9, P14, wrap next st
and turn.
Row 5: K14, P9, K1, (P1, K1) 18 (18: 20: 20:
22: 22) times, P9, K14, P9, inc once in each
of next 7 sts, wrap next st and turn.
Row 6: (P14, K9) twice, K1, (P1, K1) 18 (18:
20: 20: 22: 22) times, (K9, P14) twice, wrap
next st and turn.
Row 7: (K14, P9) twice, P1, (K1, P1) 18 (18:
20: 20: 22: 22) times, (P9, K14) twice, P9,
wrap next st and turn.
Row 8: K9, (P14, K9) twice, P1, (K1, P1)
18 (18: 20: 20: 22: 22) times, (K9, P14)
twice, K9, wrap next st and turn.
Row 9: P9, (K14, P9) twice, K1, (P1, K1)
18 (18: 20: 20: 22: 22) times, (P9, K14)
twice, P9, (K1, P1) 6 (8: 8: 10: 10: 13) times,
K1 (0: 1: 0: 1: 1).
Row 10: K1 (0: 1: 0: 1: 1), (P1, K1) 6 (8: 8:
10: 10: 13) times, K9, (P14, K9) twice, K1,
(P1, K1) 18 (18: 20: 20: 22: 22) times, (K9,
P14) twice, K9, (K1, P1) 6 (8: 8: 10: 10: 13)
times, K1 (0: 1: 0: 1: 1).
173 (179: 185: 191: 197: 209) sts.
These 10 rows complete hem shaping.
Now work in patt as folls:
Row 1 (RS): P1 (0: 1: 0: 1: 1), (K1, P1) 6 (8:
8: 10: 10: 13) times, P9, (K14, P9) twice, P1,
(K1, P1) 18 (18: 20: 20: 22: 22) times, (P9,
K14) twice, P9, (P1, K1) 6 (8: 8: 10: 10: 13)
times, P1 (0: 1: 0: 1: 1).

Row 2: P1 (0: 1: 0: 1: 1), (K1, P1) 6 (8: 8: 10:
10: 13) times, K9, (P14, K9) twice, P1, (K1,
P1) 18 (18: 20: 20: 22: 22) times, (K9, P14)
twice, K9, (P1, K1) 6 (8: 8: 10: 10: 13) times,
P1 (0: 1: 0: 1: 1).
Row 3: K1 (0: 1: 0: 1: 1), (P1, K1) 6 (8: 8: 10:
10: 13) times, P9, (K14, P9) twice, K1, (P1,
K1) 18 (18: 20: 20: 22: 22) times, (P9, K14)
twice, P9, (K1, P1) 6 (8: 8: 10: 10: 13) times,
K1 (0: 1: 0: 1: 1).
Row 4: K1 (0: 1: 0: 1: 1), (P1, K1) 6 (8: 8: 10:
10: 13) times, place marker on needle, K9,
(P14, K9) twice, place marker on needle, K1,
(P1, K1) 18 (18: 20: 20: 22: 22) times, place
marker on needle, (K9, P14) twice, K9, place
marker on needle, (K1, P1) 6 (8: 8: 10: 10:
13) times, K1 (0: 1: 0: 1: 1).
These 4 rows set the sts – 2 cable panels
of 55 sts between each pair of markers
and centre and side sts in double moss st.
Keeping sts correct as now set, cont
as folls:
Work 8 rows, dec 1 st at each end of 3rd
of these rows and ending with a WS row.
171 (177: 183: 189: 195: 207) sts.
Shape peplum
Row 1 (RS): Work 2 tog, *patt to marker,
slip marker to right needle, P2tog tbl, P5,
P2tog, C14B, P2tog tbl, P5, P2tog, C14F,
P2tog tbl, P5, P2tog, slip marker to right
needle, rep from * once more, patt to last
2 sts, work 2 tog.
157 (163: 169: 175: 181: 193) sts.
Noting that there are now only 7 sts in rev st
st between the cables (instead of 9 sts) cont
as folls:
Work 17 rows, dec 1 st at each end of 6th
and foll 6th row and ending with a WS row.
153 (159: 165: 171: 177: 189) sts.
Row 19: Work 2 tog, *patt to marker,
slip marker to right needle, P2tog tbl,
P3, P2tog, slip next 7 sts onto cn and
leave at back of work, K5, K2tog, then
K2tog, K5 from cn, P2tog tbl, P3, P2tog,
slip next 7 sts onto cn and leave at front
of work, K5, K2tog, then K2tog, K5 from
cn, P2tog tbl, P3, P2tog, slip marker to
right needle, rep from * once more, patt
to last 2 sts, work 2 tog.
131 (137: 143: 149: 155: 167) sts.

Noting that there are now only 5 sts in rev st st between the cables (instead of 7 sts) and only 12 sts in cables (instead of 14 sts) cont as folls:

Work 7 rows, dec 1 st at each end of 6th of these rows and ending with a WS row.
129 (135: 141: 147: 153: 165) sts.
Row 27: *Patt to marker, slip marker to right needle, (P2tog tbl, P1, P2tog, K12) twice, P2tog tbl, P1, P2tog, slip marker to right needle, rep from * once more, patt to end.
117 (123: 129: 135: 141: 153) sts.
Noting that there are now only 3 sts in rev st st between the cables (instead of 5 sts) cont as folls:

Work 7 rows, dec 1 st at each end of 4th of these rows and ending with a WS row.
115 (121: 127: 133: 139: 151) sts.
Row 35: Work 2 tog, *patt to marker, slip marker to right needle, P3tog, slip next 6 sts onto cn and leave at back of work, K4, K2tog, then K2tog, K4 from cn, P3tog, slip next 6 sts onto cn and leave at front of work, K4, K2tog, then K2tog, K4 from cn, P3tog, slip marker to right needle, rep from * once more, patt to last 2 sts, work 2 tog.
93 (99: 105: 111: 117: 129) sts.
These 35 rows complete peplum shaping.
Change to 3¼mm (US 3) needles.
Now work in patt as folls:
Row 1 (WS): *Patt to marker, slip marker onto right needle, (K1, P10) twice, K1, slip marker onto right needle, rep from * once more, patt to end.
Row 2: *Patt to marker, slip marker onto right needle, (P1, K10) twice, P1, slip marker onto right needle, rep from * once more, patt to end.
Rows 3 to 10: As rows 1 and 2, 4 times.
Row 11: As row 1.
Row 12: *Patt to marker, slip marker onto right needle, P1, C10B, P1, C10F, P1, slip marker onto right needle, rep from * once more, patt to end.
These 12 rows form patt for rest of back.
Keeping patt correct, cont as folls:
Work 1 row, ending with a WS row.
Change to 3¾mm (US 5) needles.
Cont in patt, inc 1 st at each end of 3rd and 9 foll 6th rows, taking inc sts into double moss st. 113 (119: 125: 131: 137: 149) sts.
Work 7 (7: 11: 11: 11: 11) rows, ending with a WS row.
Shape armholes
Keeping patt correct, cast off 4 (5: 5: 6: 6: 7) sts at beg of next 2 rows.
105 (109: 115: 119: 125: 135) sts.

Dec 1 st at each end of next 5 (5: 7: 7: 9: 11) rows, then on foll 1 (2: 2: 2: 2: 3) alt rows, then on foll 4th row.
91 (93: 95: 99: 101: 105) sts.
Cont straight until armhole measures 18 (19: 19: 20: 21: 22) cm, ending with a WS row.
Shape shoulders and back neck
Cast off 10 (10: 10: 10: 11: 11) sts at beg of next 2 rows. 71 (73: 75: 79: 79: 83) sts.
Next row (RS): Cast off 10 (10: 10: 10: 11: 11) sts, patt until there are 13 (13: 14: 15: 14: 15) sts on right needle and turn, leaving rem sts on a holder.
Work each side of neck separately.
Cast off 4 sts at beg of next row.
Cast off rem 9 (9: 10: 11: 10: 11) sts.
With RS facing, rejoin yarn to rem sts, cast off centre 25 (27: 27: 29: 29: 31) sts, patt to end.
Complete to match first side, reversing shapings.

LEFT FRONT
Cast on 83 (86: 89: 92: 95: 101) sts using 3¾mm (US 5) needles.
Row 1 (RS): K1 (0: 1: 0: 1: 1), (P1, K1) 6 (8: 8: 10: 10: 13) times, wrap next st and turn.
Row 2: (K1, P1) 6 (8: 8: 10: 10: 13) times, K1 (0: 1: 0: 1: 1).
Row 3: P1 (0: 1: 0: 1: 1), (K1, P1) 6 (8: 8: 10: 10: 13) times, P9, wrap next st and turn.
Row 4: K9, (P1, K1) 6 (8: 8: 10: 10: 13) times, P1 (0: 1: 0: 1: 1).
Row 5: K1 (0: 1: 0: 1: 1), (P1, K1) 6 (8: 8: 10: 10: 13) times, P9, inc once in each of next 7 sts, P9, wrap next st and turn.
Row 6: K9, P14, K9, (K1, P1) 6 (8: 8: 10: 10: 13) times, K1 (0: 1: 0: 1: 1).
Row 7: P1 (0: 1: 0: 1: 1), (K1, P1) 6 (8: 8: 10: 10: 13) times, P9, K14, P9, inc once in each of next 7 sts, P9, wrap next st and turn.
Row 8: (K9, P14) twice, K9, (P1, K1) 6 (8: 8: 10: 10: 13) times, P1 (0: 1: 0: 1: 1).
Row 9: Work 2 tog, K1 (0: 1: 0: 1: 1), (P1, K1) 5 (7: 7: 9: 9: 12) times, (P9, K14) twice, P9, (K1, P1) 9 (9: 10: 10: 11: 11) times, P1, (P1, K1) 5 times.
Row 10: (K1, P1) 5 times, K1, (P1, K1) 9 (9: 10: 10: 11: 11) times, (K9, P14) twice, K9, (K1, P1) 6 (7: 8: 9: 10: 13) times, P0 (1: 0: 1: 0: 0). 96 (99: 102: 105: 108: 114) sts.
These 10 rows complete hem shaping.
Now work in patt as folls:
Row 1 (RS): P0 (1: 0: 1: 0: 0), (K1, P1) 6 (7: 8: 9: 10: 13) times, (P9, K14) twice, P9, (P1, K1) 9 (9: 10: 10: 11: 11) times, P1, (P1, K1) 5 times.

Row 2: (K1, P1) 5 times, K1, (K1, P1) 9 (9: 10: 10: 11: 11) times, (K9, P14) twice, K9, (P1, K1) 6 (7: 8: 9: 10: 13) times, P0 (1: 0: 1: 0: 0).
Row 3: K0 (1: 0: 1: 0: 0), (P1, K1) 6 (7: 8: 9: 10: 13) times, (P9, K14) twice, P9, (K1, P1) 9 (9: 10: 10: 11: 11) times, P1, (P1, K1) 5 times.
Row 4: (K1, P1) 5 times, K1, (P1, K1) 9 (9: 10: 10: 11: 11) times, place marker on needle, (K9, P14) twice, K9, place marker on needle, (K1, P1) 6 (7: 8: 9: 10: 13) times, P0 (1: 0: 1: 0: 0).
These 4 rows set the sts – cable panel of 55 sts between each marker with sts either side of these sts in double moss st, and front opening edge sts in moss st.
Keeping sts correct as now set, cont as folls:
Shape peplum
Row 1 (RS): Work 2 tog, patt to marker, slip marker to right needle, P2tog tbl, P5, P2tog, C14B, P2tog tbl, P5, P2tog, C14F, P2tog tbl, P5, P2tog, slip marker to right needle, patt to end. 89 (92: 95: 98: 101: 107) sts.
Noting that there are now only 7 sts in rev st st between the cables (instead of 9 sts) cont as folls:
Work 17 rows, dec 1 st at beg of 6th and foll 6th row and ending with a WS row.
87 (90: 93: 96: 99: 105) sts.
Row 19: Work 2 tog, patt to marker, slip marker to right needle, P2tog tbl, P3, P2tog, slip next 7 sts onto cn and leave at back of work, K5, K2tog, then K2tog, K5 from cn, P2tog tbl, P3, P2tog, slip next 7 sts onto cn and leave at front of work, K5, K2tog, then K2tog, K5 from cn, P2tog tbl, P3, P2tog, slip marker to right needle, patt to end.
76 (79: 82: 85: 88: 94) sts.
Noting that there are now only 5 sts in rev st st between the cables (instead of 7 sts) and only 12 sts in cables (instead of 14 sts) cont as folls:
Work 7 rows, dec 1 st at beg of 6th of these rows and ending with a WS row.
75 (78: 81: 84: 87: 93) sts.
Row 27: Patt to marker, slip marker to right needle, (P2tog tbl, P1, P2tog, K12) twice, P2tog tbl, P1, P2tog, slip marker to right needle, patt to end.
69 (72: 75: 78: 81: 87) sts.
Noting that there are now only 3 sts in rev st st between the cables (instead of 5 sts) cont as folls:
Work 7 rows, dec 1 st at beg of 4th of these rows and ending with a WS row.
68 (71: 74: 77: 80: 86) sts.

Row 35: Work 2 tog, patt to marker, slip marker to right needle, P3tog, slip next 6 sts onto cn and leave at back of work, K4, K2tog, then K2tog, K4 from cn, P3tog, slip next 6 sts onto cn and leave at front of work, K4, K2tog, then K2tog, K4 from cn, P3tog, slip marker to right needle, patt to end. 57 (60: 63: 66: 69: 75) sts. These 35 rows complete peplum shaping. Change to 3¼mm (US 3) needles.

Now work in patt as folls:

Row 1 (WS): Patt to marker, slip marker onto right needle, (K1, P10) twice, K1, slip marker onto right needle, patt to end.

Row 2: Patt to marker, slip marker onto right needle, (P1, K10) twice, P1, slip marker onto right needle, patt to end.

Rows 3 to 10: As rows 1 and 2, 4 times.

Row 11: As row 1.

Row 12: Patt to marker, slip marker onto right needle, P1, C10B, P1, C10F, P1, slip marker onto right needle, patt to end.

These 12 rows form patt for rest of left front. Keeping patt correct, cont as folls:

Work 1 row, ending with a WS row.

Change to 3¾mm (US 5) needles.

Cont in patt, inc 1 st at beg of 3rd and 9 foll 6th rows, taking inc sts into double moss st. 67 (70: 73: 76: 79: 85) sts.

Work 7 (7: 11: 11: 11: 11) rows, ending with a WS row.

Shape armhole

Keeping patt correct, cast off 4 (5: 5: 6: 6: 7) sts at beg of next row.

63 (65: 68: 70: 73: 78) sts.

Work 1 row.

Dec 1 st at armhole edge of next 5 (5: 7: 7: 9: 11) rows, then on foll 1 (2: 2: 2: 2: 3) alt rows, then on foll 4th row.

56 (57: 58: 60: 61: 63) sts.

Cont straight until 18 (18: 18: 22: 22: 22) rows less have been worked than on back to beg of shoulder shaping, ending with a WS row.

Shape neck

Next row (RS): Patt 39 (39: 40: 42: 43: 44) sts and turn, leaving rem 17 (18: 18: 18: 18: 19) sts on a holder.

Keeping patt correct, dec 1 st at neck edge of next 6 rows, then on foll 3 alt rows, then on 1 (1: 1: 2: 2: 2) foll 4th rows.

29 (29: 30: 31: 32: 33) sts.

Work 1 row, ending with a WS row.

Shape shoulder

Cast off 10 (10: 10: 10: 11: 11) sts at beg of next and foll alt row.

Work 1 row.

Cast off rem 9 (9: 10: 11: 10: 11) sts.

Mark positions for 6 buttons along left front opening edge – first to come in row 6 of waist section worked on 3¼mm (US 3) needles, last to come just above neck shaping, and rem 4 buttons evenly spaced between.

RIGHT FRONT

Cast on 83 (86: 89: 92: 95: 101) sts using 3¾mm (US 5) needles.

Row 1 (RS): (K1, P1) 5 times, P1, (P1, K1) 9 (9: 10: 10: 11: 11) times, P9, (inc once in each of next 7 sts, P9) twice, (K1, P1) 6 (8: 8: 10: 10: 13) times, K1 (0: 1: 0: 1: 1).

Row 2: K1 (0: 1: 0: 1: 1), (P1, K1) 6 (8: 8: 10: 10: 13) times, wrap next st and turn.

Row 3: (P1, K1) 6 (8: 8: 10: 10: 13) times, P1 (0: 1: 0: 1: 1).

Row 4: P1 (0: 1: 0: 1: 1), (K1, P1) 6 (8: 8: 10: 10: 13) times, K9, wrap next st and turn.

Row 5: P9, (K1, P1) 6 (8: 8: 10: 10: 13) times, K1 (0: 1: 0: 1: 1).

Row 6: K1 (0: 1: 0: 1: 1), (P1, K1) 6 (8: 8: 10: 10: 13) times, K9, P14, K9, wrap next st and turn.

Row 7: P9, K14, P9, (P1, K1) 6 (8: 8: 10: 10: 13) times, P1 (0: 1: 0: 1: 1).

Row 8: P1 (0: 1: 0: 1: 1), (K1, P1) 6 (8: 8: 10: 10: 13) times, K9, (P14, K9) twice, wrap next st and turn.

Row 9: (P9, K14) twice, P9, (K1, P1) 5 (7: 7: 9: 9: 12) times, K1 (0: 1: 0: 1: 1), work 2 tog.

Row 10: K0 (1: 0: 1: 0: 0), (P1, K1) 6 (7: 8: 9: 10: 13) times, K9, P14, K9, (P1, K1) 9 (9: 10: 10: 11: 11) times, K1, (P1, K1) 5 times. 96 (99: 102: 105: 108: 114) sts.

These 10 rows complete hem shaping.

Now work in patt as folls:

Row 1 (RS): (K1, P1) 5 times, P1, (K1, P1) 9 (9: 10: 10: 11: 11) times, (P9, K14) twice, P9, (P1, K1) 6 (7: 8: 9: 10: 13) times, P0 (1: 0: 1: 0: 0).

Row 2: P0 (1: 0: 1: 0: 0), (K1, P1) 6 (7: 8: 9: 10: 13) times, (K9, P14) twice, K9, (P1, K1) 9 (9: 10: 10: 11: 11) times, K1, (P1, K1) 5 times.

Row 3: (K1, P1) 5 times, P1, (P1, K1) 9 (9: 10: 10: 11: 11) times, (P9, K14) twice, P9, (K1, P1) 6 (7: 8: 9: 10: 13) times, K0 (1: 0: 1: 0: 0).

Row 4: P0 (1: 0: 1: 0: 0), (P1, K1) 6 (7: 8: 9: 10: 13) times, place marker on needle, (K9, P14) twice, K9, place marker on needle, (K1, P1) 9 (9: 10: 10: 11: 11) times, K1, (P1, K1) 5 times.

These 4 rows set the sts – cable panel of 55 sts between each marker with sts either side of these sts in double moss st, and front opening edge sts in moss st.

Keeping sts correct as now set, cont as folls:

Shape peplum

Row 1 (RS): Patt to marker, slip marker to right needle, P2tog tbl, P5, P2tog, C14B, P2tog tbl, P5, P2tog, C14F, P2tog tbl, P5, P2tog, slip marker to right needle, patt to last 2 sts, work 2 tog.

89 (92: 95: 98: 101: 107) sts.

Noting that there are now only 7 sts in rev st st between the cables (instead of 9 sts) cont as folls:

Work 17 rows, dec 1 st at end of 6th and foll 6th row and ending with a WS row.

87 (90: 93: 96: 99: 105) sts.

Row 19: Patt to marker, slip marker to right needle, P2tog tbl, P3, P2tog, slip next 7 sts onto cn and leave at back of work, K5, K2tog, then K2tog, K5 from cn, P2tog tbl, P3, P2tog, slip next 7 sts onto cn and leave at front of work, K5, K2tog, then K2tog, K5 from cn, P2tog tbl, P3, P2tog, slip marker to right needle, patt to last 2 sts, work 2 tog.

76 (79: 82: 85: 88: 94) sts.

Noting that there are now only 5 sts in rev st st between the cables (instead of 7 sts) and only 12 sts in cables (instead of 14 sts) cont as folls:

Work 7 rows, dec 1 st at end of 6th of these rows and ending with a WS row.

75 (78: 81: 84: 87: 93) sts.

Row 27: Patt to marker, slip marker to right needle, (P2tog tbl, P1, P2tog, K12) twice, P2tog tbl, P1, P2tog, slip marker to right needle, patt to end. 69 (72: 75: 78: 81: 87) sts.

Noting that there are now only 3 sts in rev st st between the cables (instead of 5 sts) cont as folls:

Work 7 rows, dec 1 st at end of 4th of these rows and ending with a WS row.

68 (71: 74: 77: 80: 86) sts.

Row 35: Patt to marker, slip marker to right needle, P3tog, slip next 6 sts onto cn and leave at back of work, K4, K2tog, then K2tog, K4 from cn, P3tog, slip next 6 sts onto cn and leave at front of work, K4, K2tog, then K2tog, K4 from cn, P3tog, slip marker to right needle, patt to last 2 sts, work 2 tog.

57 (60: 63: 66: 69: 75) sts.

These 35 rows complete peplum shaping. Change to 3¼mm (US 3) needles.

Now work in patt as folls:

Row 1 (WS): Patt to marker, slip marker onto right needle, (K1, P10) twice, K1, slip marker onto right needle, patt to end.

Row 2: Patt to marker, slip marker onto right needle, (P1, K10) twice, P1, slip marker onto right needle, patt to end.

Rows 3 and 4: As rows 1 and 2.
Row 5: As row 1.
Row 6 (buttonhole row) (RS): Patt 4 sts, cast off 2 sts (to make a buttonhole – cast on 2 sts over these cast-off sts on next row), patt to end.
Rows 7 to 10: As rows 1 and 2, twice.
Row 11: As row 1.
Row 12: Patt to marker, slip marker onto right needle, P1, C10B, P1, C10F, P1, slip marker onto right needle, patt to end.
These 12 rows form patt for rest of right front.
Working a further 4 buttonholes as set by row 6 to correspond with positions marked for buttons on left front, complete to match left front, reversing shapings and working first row of neck shaping at folls:

Shape neck
Next row (RS): Patt 17 (18: 18: 18: 18: 19) sts and slip these sts onto a holder, patt to end. 39 (39: 40: 42: 43: 44) sts.

LEFT SLEEVE
Front sleeve
Cast on 28 (29: 30: 32: 33: 34) sts using 3¼mm (US 3) needles.
Work in garter st for 3 rows, ending with a **RS** row.
Change to 3¾mm (US 9) needles.
Row 4 (WS): P0 (1: 0: 0: 1: 0), *K1, P1, rep from * to end.
Row 5: *P1, K1, rep from * to last 0 (1: 0: 0: 1: 0) st, P0 (1: 0: 0: 1: 0).
Row 6: K0 (1: 0: 0: 1: 0), *P1, K1, rep from * to end.
Row 7: *K1, P1, rep from * to last 0 (1: 0: 0: 1: 0) st, K0 (1: 0: 0: 1: 0).
These 4 rows form double moss st.
Cont in double moss st, inc 1 st at end of 2nd (2nd: 2nd: 4th: 4th: 2nd) and 2 foll 10th (10th: 12th: 12th: 12th: 12th) rows. 31 (32: 33: 35: 36: 37) sts.
Work 7 (7: 3: 1: 1: 3) rows, ending with a WS row.
Break yarn and leave sts on a holder.
Back sleeve
Cast on 28 (29: 30: 32: 33: 34) sts using 3¼mm (US 3) needles.
Work in garter st for 3 rows, ending with a **RS** row.
Change to 3¾mm (US 9) needles.
Row 4 (WS): *P1, K1, rep from * to last 0 (1: 0: 0: 1: 0) st, P0 (1: 0: 0: 1: 0).
Row 5: P0 (1: 0: 0: 1: 0), *K1, P1, rep from * to end.
Row 6: *K1, P1, rep from * to last 0 (1: 0: 0: 1: 0) st, K0 (1: 0: 0: 1: 0).

Row 7: K0 (1: 0: 0: 1: 0), *P1, K1, rep from * to end.
These 4 rows form double moss st.
Cont in double moss st, inc 1 st at beg of 2nd (2nd: 2nd: 4th: 4th: 2nd) and 2 foll 10th (10th: 12th: 12th: 12th: 12th) rows. 31 (32: 33: 35: 36: 37) sts.
Work 7 (7: 3: 1: 1: 3) rows, ending with a WS row.

Join sections
Next row (RS): Patt to last 7 sts of sleeve back, holding WS of sleeve front against RS of sleeve back, work tog first st of sleeve front with next st of sleeve back, (work tog next st of sleeve front with next st of sleeve back) 6 times, patt to end. 55 (57: 59: 63: 65: 67) sts.
**Cont in patt, inc 1 st at each end of 2nd (2nd: 8th: 10th: 10th: 8th) and every foll 12th (10th: 12th: 12th: 12th: 12th) row to 73 (67: 77: 79: 77: 87) sts, then on every foll - (12th: -: 14th: 14th: -) row until there are - (77: -: 81: 83: -) sts.
Cont straight until sleeve measures 45 (46: 47: 48: 49: 50) cm, ending with a WS row.

Shape top
Keeping patt correct, cast off 4 (5: 5: 6: 6: 7) sts at beg of next 2 rows.
65 (67: 67: 69: 71: 73) sts.
Dec 1 st at each end of next 3 rows, then on foll alt row, then on foll 4th row, then on 3 foll 6th rows. 49 (51: 51: 53: 55: 57) sts.
Work 3 rows.
Dec 1 st at each end of next and foll 4th row, then on every foll alt row to 41 sts, then on foll 5 rows, ending with a WS row.
Cast off rem 31 sts.

RIGHT SLEEVE
Back sleeve
Work as given for front sleeve of left sleeve.
Front sleeve
Work as given for back sleeve of left sleeve.
Join sections
Next row (RS): Patt to last 7 sts of sleeve front, holding WS of sleeve front against RS of sleeve back, work tog next st of sleeve front with first st of sleeve back, (work tog next st of sleeve front with next st of sleeve back) 6 times, patt to end.
55 (57: 59: 63: 65: 67) sts.
Complete as given for left sleeve from **.

MAKING UP
Pin the pieces out and steam gently without allowing the iron to touch the yarn.
Join both shoulder seams using back stitch or mattress stitch if preferred.

Neckband
With RS facing and using 3¼mm (US 3) needles, slip 17 (18: 18: 18: 18: 19) sts from right front holder onto right needle, rejoin yarn and pick up and knit 23 (23: 23: 27: 27: 27) sts up right side of neck, 33 (35: 35: 37: 37: 39) sts from back, and 23 (23: 23: 27: 27: 27) sts down left side of neck, then patt across 17 (18: 18: 18: 18: 19) sts on left front holder.
113 (117: 117: 127: 127: 131) sts.
Next row (WS): Patt first 11 sts as set by left front, work in double moss st as set by rem sts of left front holder sts to last 11 sts, patt to end as set by right front sts.
Keeping sts correct as now set, cont as folls:
Next row: Patt 4 sts, cast off 2 sts (to make 6th buttonhole – cast on 2 sts over these cast-off sts on next row), patt to end.
Work a further 6 rows, ending with a **RS** row.
Cast off in patt (on WS).
Join side seams. Join sleeve seams. Insert sleeves into armholes. Sew on buttons, attaching 3 small buttons to each cuff through edges of both sleeve front and back as in photograph.

40.5 (43: 45.5: 48: 50.5: 55) cm
16 (17: 18: 19: 20: 21½) in

55 (56: 57: 58: 59: 60) cm
21½ (22: 22½: 23: 23¼: 23½) in

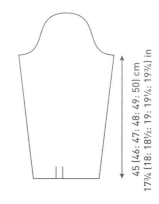

45 (46: 47: 48: 49: 50) cm
17¾ (18: 18½: 19: 19¼: 19¾) in

CHAISE

THE ULTIMATE CLASSIC SWEATER

Recommendation

Suitable for the knitter with a little experience
Please see pages 21, 22 & 23 for photographs.

	XS	S	M	L	XL	XXL	
To fit	**81**	**86**	**91**	**97**	**102**	**109**	**cm**
bust	32	34	36	38	40	43	in

Rowan Pure Cashmere DK

	11	11	12	13	13	14	x 25gm

Photographed in Greige

Needles

1 pair 3mm (no 11) (US 2/3) needles
1 pair 3¼mm (no 10) (US 3) needles

Tension

27 sts and 37 rows to 10 cm measured over
stocking stitch using 3¼mm (US 3) needles.

BACK

Cast on 107 (115: 121: 127: 135: 147) sts
using 3mm (US 2/3) needles.
Work in garter st for 3 rows, ending with a **RS** row.
Row 4 (WS): P1, *K1, P1, rep from * to end.
Row 5: As row 4.
Last 2 rows form moss st.
Work in moss st for a further 9 rows, dec 1 st at
each end of 6th of these rows and ending with
a WS row. 105 (113: 119: 125: 133: 145) sts.
Change to 3¼mm (US 3) needles.
Beg with a K row, work in st st as folls:
Work 4 rows, ending with a WS row.
Next row (dec) (RS): K2, K2tog, K to last 4 sts,
K2tog tbl, K2.**
Working all side seam decreases as set by last
row, dec 1 st at each end of 8th and 2 foll 8th
rows, then on 2 foll 6th rows.
93 (101: 107: 113: 121: 133) sts.
***Work 13 rows, ending with a WS row.
Next row (inc) (RS): K3, M1, K to last 3 sts,
M1, K3.
Working all side seam increases as set by last
row, inc 1 st at each end of 10th and foll 10th
row, then on 5 foll 8th rows.
109 (117: 123: 129: 137: 149) sts.
Cont straight until back measures 37 (37: 38:
38: 38: 38) cm, ending with a WS row.
Shape armholes
Cast off 4 (5: 5: 6: 6: 7) sts at beg of next
2 rows. 101 (107: 113: 117: 125: 135) sts.
Dec 1 st at each end of next 3 (3: 5: 5: 7: 9)
rows, then on foll 3 (5: 5: 5: 6: 8) alt rows, then
on 2 foll 4th rows.
85 (87: 89: 93: 95: 97) sts.
Cont straight until armhole measures 18 (19:
19: 20: 21: 22) cm, ending with a WS row.
Shape shoulders and back neck
Cast off 6 (6: 6: 7: 7: 7) sts at beg of next
2 rows. 73 (75: 77: 79: 81: 83) sts.
Next row (RS): Cast off 6 (6: 6: 7: 7: 7) sts, K
until there are 10 (10: 11: 10: 11: 12) sts on
right needle and turn, leaving rem sts on
a holder.
Work each side of neck separately.
Cast off 4 sts at beg of next row.
Cast off rem 6 (6: 7: 6: 7: 8) sts.
With RS facing, rejoin yarn to rem sts, cast off
centre 41 (43: 43: 45: 45: 45) sts, K to end.
Complete to match first side, rev shapings.

POCKET LININGS (make 2)

Cast on 23 (23: 25: 25: 27: 27) sts using
3¼mm (US 3) needles.
Beg with a K row, work in st st for 22 rows,
ending with a WS row.
Break yarn and leave sts on a holder.

FRONT

Work as given for back to **.
Working all side seam decreases as set
by last row, dec 1 st at each end of 8th and
foll 8th row.
99 (107: 113: 119: 127: 139) sts.
Work 1 row, ending with a WS row.
Place pockets
Next row (RS): K12 (15: 15: 17: 18: 23),
slip next 23 (23: 25: 25: 27: 27) sts onto
a holder and, in their place, K across
23 (23: 25: 25: 27: 27) sts of first pocket
lining, K29 (31: 33: 35: 37: 39), slip next
23 (23: 25: 25: 27: 27) sts onto another
holder and, in their place, K across
23 (23: 25: 25: 27: 27) sts of second
pocket lining, K12 (15: 15: 17: 18: 23).
Dec 1 st at each end of 6th and 2 foll
6th rows.
93 (101: 107: 113: 121: 133) sts.
Work as given for back from *** until
26 (26: 26: 30: 30: 30) rows less have
been worked than on back to beg of
shoulder shaping, ending with a WS row.
Shape front neck
Next row (RS): K31 (31: 32: 34: 35: 36)
and turn, leaving rem sts on a holder.
Work each side of neck separately.
Dec 1 st at neck edge of next 8 rows, then
on foll 3 alt rows, then on 2 (2: 2: 3: 3: 3)
foll 4th rows.
18 (18: 19: 20: 21: 22) sts.
Work 3 rows, ending with a WS row.
Shape shoulder
Cast off 6 (6: 6: 7: 7: 7) sts at beg of next
and foll alt row.
Work 1 row.
Cast off rem 6 (6: 7: 6: 7: 8) sts.
With RS facing, rejoin yarn to rem sts,
cast off centre 23 (25: 25: 25: 25: 25) sts,
K to end.
Complete to match first side, reversing
shapings.

SLEEVES (both alike)

Cast on 51 (53: 53: 55: 57: 59) sts using 3mm (US 2/3) needles.
Work in garter st for 3 rows, ending with a **RS** row.
Work in moss st as given for back for 11 rows, inc 1 st at each end of 10th of these rows and ending with a WS row.
53 (55: 55: 57: 59: 61) sts.
Change to 3¼mm (US 3) needles.
Beg with a K row and working all sleeve increases in same way as side seam increases, work in st st, shaping sides by inc 1 st at each end of 9th [7th: 7th: 7th: 7th: 7th] and every foll 10th (8th: 8th: 8th: 8th: 8th) row to 77 (59: 59: 67: 65: 73) sts, then on every foll 12th (10th: 10th: 10th: 10th: 10th) row until there are 79 (83: 83: 87: 89: 93) sts.
Cont straight until sleeve measures 44 (45: 45: 46: 47: 48) cm, ending with a WS row.

Shape top

Cast off 4 (5: 5: 6: 6: 7) sts at beg of next 2 rows. 71 (73: 73: 75: 77: 79) sts.
Dec 1 st at each end of next 3 rows, then on foll alt row, then on 8 foll 4th rows.
47 (49: 49: 51: 53: 55) sts.
Work 1 row.
Dec 1 st at each end of next and every foll alt row to 41 sts, then on foll 5 rows, ending with a WS row.
Cast off rem 31 sts.

MAKING UP

Pin the pieces out and steam gently without allowing the iron to touch the yarn.
Join right shoulder seam using back stitch or mattress stitch if preferred.

Neckband

With RS facing and using 3mm (US 2/3) needles, pick up and knit 30 (30: 30: 33: 33: 33) sts down left side of neck, 23 (25: 25: 25: 25: 25) sts from front, 30 (30: 30: 33: 33: 33) sts up right side of neck, then 50 (52: 52: 54: 54: 54) sts from back.
133 (137: 137: 145: 145: 145) sts.
Work in moss st as given for back for 7 rows, ending a WS row.
Work in garter st for 3 rows, ending with a **RS** row.
Cast off knitwise (on **WS**).

Pocket tops (both alike)

Slip 23 (23: 25: 25: 27: 27) sts from pocket holder onto 3mm (US 2/3) needles and rejoin yarn with RS facing.
Work in moss st as given for back for 6 rows, ending a WS row.

Work in garter st for 3 rows, ending with a **RS** row.
Cast off knitwise (on **WS**).
Join left shoulder and neckband seam.
Join side seams. Join sleeve seams. Insert sleeves into armholes. Sew pocket linings in place on inside, then neatly sew down ends of pocket tops.

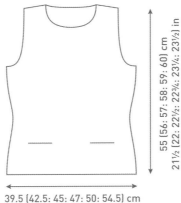

39.5 (42.5: 45: 47: 50: 54.5) cm
15½ (16¾: 17¾: 18½: 19½: 21½) in

55 (56: 57: 58: 59: 60) cm
21½ (22: 22½: 22¾: 23¼: 23½) in

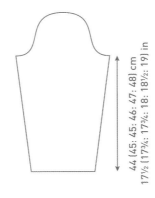

44 (45: 45: 46: 47: 48) cm
17½ (17¾: 17¾: 18: 18½: 19) in

RYDER

TAILORED CABLED SWEATER WITH BUTTON DETAIL

Recommendation

Suitable for the knitter with a little experience
Please see pages 17 & 18 for photographs.

	XS	S	M	L	XL	XXL	
To fit	**81**	**86**	**91**	**97**	**102**	**109**	**cm**
bust	32	34	36	38	40	43	in

Rowan Wool Cotton

| | 12 | 13 | 13 | 14 | 14 | 15 | x 50gm |

Photographed in Tender

Needles

1 pair 3¼mm (no 10) (US 3) needles
1 pair 3¾mm (no 9) (US 5) needles
Cable needle

Buttons · 6

Tension

23 sts and 38 rows to 10 cm measured over
moss stitch using 3¾mm (US 5) needles.
Note that on the front and back the cables will
alter the row tension to 36 rows to 10 cm.

SPECIAL ABBREVIATIONS

C10B = slip next 5 sts onto cable needle and
leave at back of work, K5, then K5 from cable
needle; **C10F** = slip next 5 sts onto cable
needle and leave at front of work, K5, then
K5 from cable needle; **C14B** = slip next 7 sts
onto cable needle and leave at back of work,
K7, then K7 from cable needle; **C14F** = slip
next 7 sts onto cable needle and leave at front
of work, K7, then K7 from cable needle.

Pattern note: When casting off sts for
shoulders, work 2 sts tog across top of each
cable to avoid the shoulder edge stretching
and sagging out of shape. The number of sts
given to be cast off do NOT take into account
these decreases.

BACK

Right side panel

Cast on 72 (75: 78: 81: 84: 89) sts using
3¾mm (US 5) needles.
Row 1 (RS): K1 (0: 1: 0: 1: 0), (P1, K1) 6 (8:
8: 10: 10: 13) times, (P9, inc once in each of
next 7 sts) twice, P9, (P1, K1) 9 (9: 10: 10:
11: 11) times. 86 (89: 92: 95: 98: 103) sts.
Row 2: (K1, P1) 6 (6: 7: 7: 8: 8) times, K1,
wrap next st (by slipping next st from left
needle to right needle, taking yarn to opposite
side of work between needles and then
slipping same st back onto left needle – when
working back across wrapped sts work the
wrapped st and the wrapping loop tog as
one st) and turn.
Row 3: (K1, P1) 6 (6: 7: 7: 8: 8) times, K1.
Row 4: (K1, P1) 9 (9: 10: 10: 11: 11) times,
wrap next st and turn.
Row 5: (P1, K1) 9 (9: 10: 10: 11: 11) times.
Row 6: (K1, P1) 9 (9: 10: 10: 11: 11) times,
K9, wrap next st and turn.
Row 7: P9, (P1, K1) 9 (9: 10: 10: 11: 11)
times.
Row 8: (K1, P1) 9 (9: 10: 10: 11: 11) times,
K9, P14, wrap next st and turn.
Row 9: K14, P9, (P1, K1) 9 (9: 10: 10: 11:
11) times.
Row 10: (K1, P1) 9 (9: 10: 10: 11: 11) times,
(K9, P14) twice, wrap next st and turn.
Row 11: (K14, P9) twice, (P1, K1) 9 (9: 10:
10: 11: 11) times.
Row 12: (K1, P1) 9 (9: 10: 10: 11: 11) times,
(K9, P14) twice, K9, wrap next st and turn.
Row 13: P9, (K14, P9) twice, (P1, K1) 9 (9:
10: 10: 11: 11) times.
Row 14: (K1, P1) 9 (9: 10: 10: 11: 11) times,
(K9, P14) twice, K9, (K1, P1) 6 (8: 8: 10: 10:
13) times, K1 (0: 1: 0: 1: 0).
These 14 rows complete hem shaping and
set the sts – 2 panels of 14 sts in st st (for
cables) with 9 sts in rev st st between and at
sides of these, with edge sts in moss st.
Keeping sts correct as now set, cont as folls:
Work 12 rows, dec 1 st at beg of 7th of these
rows and ending with a WS row.
85 (88: 91: 94: 97: 102) sts.

Shape peplum

Place markers either side of the 55 sts in st st
and rev st st between the moss st panels.

Row 27 (RS): Work 2 tog, moss st to marker,
slip marker to right needle, P2tog tbl, P5, P2tog,
C14B, P2tog tbl, P5, P2tog, C14F, P2tog tbl,
P5, P2tog, slip marker to right needle, moss
st to end. 78 (81: 84: 87: 90: 95) sts.
Noting that there are now only 7 sts in rev st
st between the cables (instead of 9 sts) cont
as folls:
Work 17 rows, dec 1 st at beg of 6th and foll
6th row and ending with a WS row.
76 (79: 82: 85: 88: 93) sts.
Row 45 (RS): Work 2 tog, moss st to marker,
slip marker to right needle, P2tog tbl, P3,
P2tog, slip next 7 sts onto cn and leave at
back of work, K5, K2tog, then K2tog, K5 from
cn, P2tog tbl, P3, P2tog, slip next 7 sts onto
cn and leave at front of work, K5, K2tog, then
K2tog, K5 from cn, P2tog tbl, P3, P2tog, slip
marker to right needle, moss st to end.
65 (68: 71: 74: 77: 82) sts.
Noting that there are now only 5 sts in rev st
st between the cables (instead of 7 sts) and
only 12 sts in cables (instead of 14 sts) cont
as folls:
Work 7 rows, dec 1 st at beg of 6th of these
rows and ending with a WS row.
64 (67: 70: 73: 76: 81) sts.
Row 53 (RS): Moss st to marker, slip marker
to right needle, (P2tog tbl, P1, P2tog, K12)
twice, P2tog tbl, P1, P2tog, slip marker to
right needle, moss st to end.
58 (61: 64: 67: 70: 75) sts.
Noting that there are now only 3 sts in rev
st st between the cables (instead of 5 sts)
cont as folls:
Work 7 rows, dec 1 st at beg of 4th of these
rows and ending with a WS row.
57 (60: 63: 66: 69: 74) sts.
Row 61 (RS): Work 2 tog, moss st to marker,
slip marker to right needle, P3tog, slip next
6 sts onto cn and leave at back of work, K4,
K2tog, then K2tog, K4 from cn, P3tog, slip
next 6 sts onto cn and leave at front of work,
K4, K2tog, then K2tog, K4 from cn, P3tog,
slip marker to right needle, moss st to end.
46 (49: 52: 55: 58: 63) sts.
Noting that there is now only 1 st in rev st st
between the cables (instead of 3 sts) and only
10 sts in cables (instead of 12 sts) cont as folls:
Work 11 rows, ending with a WS row.

Next row (RS): Moss st to marker, remove marker, P1, C10B, P1, C10F, P1, remove marker, moss st to end.

Last 12 rows set the sts for rest of back – 2 cables of 10 sts with one st in rev st st between and at sides of these sts, and rem sts in moss st.

Keeping sts correct as now set and working cables on every foll 12th row from previous cables, inc 1 st at beg of 4th and 3 foll 6th rows, taking inc sts into moss st.

50 (53: 56: 59: 62: 67) sts.

Work 5 rows, ending with a WS row.

Break yarn and leave sts on a holder.

Left side panel

Cast on 72 (75: 78: 81: 84: 89) sts using 3¾mm (US 5) needles.

Row 1 (RS): K1, (P1, K1) 6 (6: 7: 7: 8: 8) times, wrap next st and turn.

Row 2: K1, (P1, K1) 6 (6: 7: 7: 8: 8) times.

Row 3: (K1, P1) 9 (9: 10: 10: 11: 11) times, wrap next st and turn.

Row 4: (P1, K1) 9 (9: 10: 10: 11: 11) times.

Row 5: (K1, P1) 9 (9: 10: 10: 11: 11) times, P9, wrap next st and turn.

Row 6: K9, (P1, K1) 9 (9: 10: 10: 11: 11) times.

Row 7: (K1, P1) 9 (9: 10: 10: 11: 11) times, P9, inc once in each of next 7 sts, wrap next st and turn.

Row 8: P14, K9, (P1, K1) 9 (9: 10: 10: 11: 11) times.

Row 9: (K1, P1) 9 (9: 10: 10: 11: 11) times, P9, K14, P9, inc once in each of next 7 sts, wrap next st and turn.

Row 10: (P14, K9) twice, (P1, K1) 9 (9: 10: 10: 11: 11) times.

Row 11: (K1, P1) 9 (9: 10: 10: 11: 11) times, (P9, K14) twice, P9, wrap next st and turn.

Row 12: K9, (P14, K9) twice, (P1, K1) 9 (9: 10: 10: 11: 11) times.

Row 13: (K1, P1) 9 (9: 10: 10: 11: 11) times, (P9, K14) twice, P9, (K1, P1) 6 (8: 8: 10: 10: 13) times, K1 (0: 1: 0: 1: 0).

86 (89: 92: 95: 98: 103) sts.

Row 14: K1 (0: 1: 0: 1: 0), (P1, K1) 6 (8: 8: 10: 10: 13) times, (K9, P14) twice, K9, (P1, K1) 9 (9: 10: 10: 11: 11) times.

These 14 rows complete hem shaping and set the sts – 2 panels of 14 sts in st st (for cables) with 9 sts in rev st st between and at sides of these, with edge sts in moss st.

Keeping sts correct as now set, cont as folls:

Work 4 rows, ending with a WS row.

Row 19 (buttonhole row) (RS): K1, P1, K2tog tbl, yfrn, P2tog (to make a buttonhole – on next row work **twice** into yfrn of previous row), patt to end.

Making a further 5 buttonholes in this way on every foll 16th row from previous buttonhole and noting that no further reference will be made to buttonholes, cont as folls:

Work 7 rows, dec 1 st at end of 2nd of these rows and ending with a WS row.

85 (88: 91: 94: 97: 102) sts.

Shape peplum

Place markers either side of the 55 sts in st st and rev st st between the moss st panels.

Row 27 (RS): Moss st to marker, slip marker to right needle, P2tog tbl, P5, P2tog, C14B, P2tog tbl, P5, P2tog, C14F, P2tog tbl, P5, P2tog, slip marker to right needle, moss st to last 2 sts, work 2 tog.

78 (81: 84: 87: 90: 95) sts.

Noting that there are now only 7 sts in rev st st between the cables (instead of 9 sts) cont as folls:

Work 17 rows, dec 1 st at end of 6th and foll 6th row and ending with a WS row.

76 (79: 82: 85: 88: 93) sts.

Row 45 (RS): Moss st to marker, slip marker to right needle, P2tog tbl, P3, P2tog, slip next 7 sts onto cn and leave at back of work, K5, K2tog, then K2tog, K5 from cn, P2tog tbl, P3, P2tog, slip next 7 sts onto cn and leave at front of work, K5, K2tog, then K2tog, K5 from cn, P2tog tbl, P3, P2tog, slip marker to right needle, moss st to last 2 sts, work 2 tog.

65 (68: 71: 74: 77: 82) sts.

Noting that there are now only 5 sts in rev st st between the cables (instead of 7 sts) and only 12 sts in cables (instead of 14 sts) cont as folls:

Work 7 rows, dec 1 st at end of 6th of these rows and ending with a WS row.

64 (67: 70: 73: 76: 81) sts.

Row 53 (RS): Moss st to marker, slip marker to right needle, (P2tog tbl, P1, P2tog, K12) twice, P2tog tbl, P1, P2tog, slip marker to right needle, moss st to end.

58 (61: 64: 67: 70: 75) sts.

Noting that there are now only 3 sts in rev st st between the cables (instead of 5 sts) cont as folls:

Work 7 rows, dec 1 st at end of 4th of these rows and ending with a WS row.

57 (60: 63: 66: 69: 74) sts.

Row 61 (RS): Moss st to marker, slip marker to right needle, P3tog, slip next 6 sts onto cn and leave at back of work, K4, K2tog, then K2tog, K4 from cn, P3tog, slip next 6 sts onto cn and leave at front of work, K4, K2tog, then K2tog, K4 from cn, P3tog, slip marker to right needle, moss st to last 2 sts, work 2 tog.

46 (49: 52: 55: 58: 63) sts.

Noting that there is now only 1 st in rev st st between the cables (instead of 3 sts) and only 10 sts in cables (instead of 12 sts) cont as folls:

Work 11 rows, ending with a WS row.

Next row (RS): Moss st to marker, remove marker, P1, C10B, P1, C10F, P1, remove marker, moss st to end.

Last 12 rows set the sts for rest of back – 2 cables of 10 sts with one st in rev st st between and at sides of these sts, and rem sts in moss st.

Keeping sts correct as now set and working cables on every foll 12th row from previous cables, inc 1 st at end of 4th and 3 foll 6th rows, taking inc sts into moss st.

50 (53: 56: 59: 62: 67) sts.

Work 5 rows, ending with a WS row.

Break yarn.

Join sections

Next row (RS): Work across 50 (53: 56: 59: 62: 67) sts of right side panel as folls: inc in first st, patt to last 7 sts, holding WS of left back panel against RS of right back panel and keeping moss st correct, work tog first st of left back panel with next st of right back panel, (work tog next st of left back panel with next st of right back panel) 6 times, patt to last st of left back panel, inc in last st.

95 (101: 107: 113: 119: 129) sts.

Cont in patt as set across all sts, inc 1 st at each end of 6th and 4 foll 6th rows.

105 (111: 117: 123: 129: 139) sts.

Measuring at centre (longest section) of back, cont straight until back measures 39 (39: 40: 40: 40: 40) cm, ending with a WS row.

Shape armholes

Keeping patt correct, cast off 3 (4: 4: 5: 5: 6) sts at beg of next 2 rows.

99 (103: 109: 113: 119: 127) sts.

Dec 1 st at each end of next 5 (5: 7: 7: 9: 11) rows, then on foll 2 (3: 3: 4: 4: 4) alt rows, then on foll 4th row. 83 (85: 87: 89: 91: 95) sts.

Cont straight until armhole measures 18 (19: 19: 20: 21: 22) cm, ending with a WS row.

Shape shoulders and back neck

Cast off 6 (6: 7: 7: 7: 7) sts at beg of next 2 rows. 71 (73: 73: 75: 77: 81) sts.

Next row (RS): Cast off 6 (6: 7: 7: 7: 7) sts, patt until there are 11 (11: 10: 10: 11: 12) sts on right needle and turn, leaving rem sts on a holder.

Work each side of neck separately.

Cast off 4 sts at beg of next row.

Cast off rem 7 (7: 6: 6: 7: 8) sts.

With RS facing, rejoin yarn to rem sts, cast off centre 37 (39: 39: 41: 41: 43) sts, patt to end.

Complete to match first side, rev shapings.

FRONT

Cast on 137 (143: 149: 155: 161: 171) sts using 3¾mm (US 5) needles.

Row 1 (RS): K1 (0: 1: 0: 1: 0), (P1, K1) 6 (8: 8: 10: 10: 13) times, (P9, inc once in each of next 7 sts) twice, P9, (P1, K1) 12 (12: 14: 14: 16: 16) times, wrap next st and turn.

Row 2: (K1, P1) 9 (9: 11: 11: 13: 13) times, K1, wrap next st and turn.

Row 3: (K1, P1) 12 (12: 14: 14: 16: 16) times, wrap next st and turn.

Row 4: (P1, K1) 14 (14: 16: 16: 18: 18) times, P1, wrap next st and turn.

Row 5: P1, (K1, P1) 14 (14: 16: 16: 18: 18) times, P9, wrap next st and turn.

Row 6: K9, (K1, P1) 14 (14: 16: 16: 18: 18) times, K10, wrap next st and turn.

Row 7: P9, (P1, K1) 14 (14: 16: 16: 18: 18) times, P10, inc once in each of next 7 sts, wrap next st and turn.

Row 8: P14, K9, (P1, K1) 14 (14: 16: 16: 18: 18) times, P1, K9, P14, wrap next st and turn.

Row 9: K14, P9, (P1, K1) 14 (14: 16: 16: 18: 18) times, P1, P9, K14, P9, inc once in each of next 7 sts, wrap next st and turn.

Row 10: (P14, K9) twice, P1, (K1, P1) 14 (14: 16: 16: 18: 18) times, (K9, P14) twice, wrap next st and turn.

Row 11: (K14, P9) twice, (P1, K1) 14 (14: 16: 16: 18: 18) times, P1, (P9, K14) twice, P9, wrap next st and turn.

Row 12: K9, (P14, K9) twice, P1, (K1, P1) 14 (14: 16: 16: 18: 18) times, (K9, P14) twice, K9, wrap next st and turn.

Row 13: P9, (K14, P9) twice, (P1, K1) 14 (14: 16: 16: 18: 18) times, P1, (P9, K14) twice, P9, (K1, P1) 6 (8: 8: 10: 10: 13) times, K1 (0: 1: 0: 1: 0).

Row 14: K1 (0: 1: 0: 1: 0), (P1, K1) 6 (8: 8: 10: 10: 13) times, (K9, P14) twice, K9, P1, (K1, P1) 14 (14: 16: 16: 18: 18) times, (K9, P14) twice, K9, (K1, P1) 6 (8: 8: 10: 10: 13) times, K1 (0: 1: 0: 1: 0).

165 (171: 177: 183: 189: 199) sts.

These 14 rows complete hem shaping and set the sts – 4 panels of 14 sts in st st (for cables) with 9 sts in rev st st between and at sides of these, with centre and edge sts in moss st.

Keeping sts correct as now set, cont as folls:
Work 12 rows, dec 1 st at each end of 7th of these rows and ending with a WS row.
163 (169: 175: 181: 187: 197) sts.

Shape peplum

Place markers either side of both of the 55 sts in st st and rev st st between the moss st panels.

Row 27 (RS): Work 2 tog, *moss st to marker, slip marker to right needle, P2tog tbl, P5, P2tog, C14B, P2tog tbl, P5, P2tog, C14F, P2tog tbl, P5, P2tog, slip marker to right needle, rep from * once more, moss st to last 2 sts, work 2 tog.
149 (155: 161: 167: 173: 183) sts.
Noting that there are now only 7 sts in rev st st between the cables (instead of 9 sts) cont as folls:
Work 17 rows, dec 1 st at each end of 6th and foll 6th row and ending with a WS row.
145 (151: 157: 163: 169: 179) sts.

Row 45 (RS): Work 2 tog, *moss st to marker, slip marker to right needle, P2tog tbl, P3, P2tog, slip next 7 sts onto cn and leave at back of work, K5, K2tog, then K2tog, K5 from cn, P2tog tbl, P3, P2tog, slip next 7 sts onto cn and leave at front of work, K5, K2tog, then K2tog, K5 from cn, P2tog tbl, P3, P2tog, slip marker to right needle, rep from * once more, moss st to last 2 sts, work 2 tog.
123 (129: 135: 141: 147: 157) sts.
Noting that there are now only 5 sts in rev st st between the cables (instead of 7 sts) and only 12 sts in cables (instead of 14 sts) cont as folls:
Work 7 rows, dec 1 st at each end of 6th of these rows and ending with a WS row.
121 (127: 133: 139: 145: 155) sts.

Row 53 (RS): *Moss st to marker, slip marker to right needle, (P2tog tbl, P1, P2tog, K12) twice, P2tog tbl, P1, P2tog, slip marker to right needle, rep from * once more, moss st to end.
109 (115: 121: 127: 133: 143) sts.
Noting that there are now only 3 sts in rev st st between the cables (instead of 5 sts) cont as folls:
Work 7 rows, dec 1 st at each end of 4th of these rows and ending with a WS row.
107 (113: 119: 125: 131: 141) sts.

Row 61 (RS): Work 2 tog, *moss st to marker, slip marker to right needle, P3tog, slip next 6 sts onto cn and leave at back of work, K4, K2tog, then K2tog, K4 from cn, P3tog, slip next 6 sts onto cn and leave at front of work, K4, K2tog, then K2tog, K4 from cn, P3tog, slip marker o right needle, rep from * once more, moss st to last 2 sts, work 2 tog.
85 (91: 97: 103: 109: 119) sts.
Noting that there is now only 1 st in rev st st between the cables (instead of 3 sts) and only 10 sts in cables (instead of 12 sts) cont as folls:
Work 11 rows, ending with a WS row.

Next row (RS): *Moss st to marker, remove marker, P1, C10B, P1, C10F, P1, remove marker, rep from * once more, moss st to end.
Last 12 rows set the sts for rest of front – 4 cables of 10 sts with one st in rev st st between and at sides of these sts, and rem sts in moss st.
Keeping sts correct as now set and working cables on every foll 12th row from previous cables, inc 1 st at each end of 4th and 9 foll 6th rows, taking inc sts into moss st.
105 (111: 117: 123: 129: 139) sts.
Cont straight until front matches back to beg of armhole shaping, ending with a WS row.

Shape armholes

Keeping patt correct, cast off 3 (4: 4: 5: 5: 6) sts at beg of next 2 rows.
99 (103: 109: 113: 119: 127) sts.
Dec 1 st at each end of next 5 (5: 7: 7: 9: 11) rows, then on foll 2 (3: 3: 4: 4: 4) alt rows, then on foll 4th row.
83 (85: 87: 89: 91: 95) sts.
Cont straight until 22 (22: 22: 26: 26: 26) rows less have been worked than on back to beg of shoulder shaping, ending with a WS row.

Shape front neck

Next row (RS): Patt 31 (31: 32: 33: 34: 35) sts and turn, leaving rem sts on a holder.
Work each side of neck separately.
Keeping patt correct, dec 1 st at neck edge of next 8 rows, then on foll 2 alt rows, then on 2 (2: 2: 3: 3: 3) foll 4th rows.
19 (19: 20: 20: 21: 22) sts.
Work 1 row, ending with a WS row.

Shape shoulder

Cast off 6 (6: 7: 7: 7: 7) sts at beg of next and foll alt row.
Work 1 row.
Cast off rem 7 (7: 6: 6: 7: 8) sts.
With RS facing, rejoin yarn to rem sts, cast off centre 21 (23: 23: 23: 23: 25) sts, patt to end.
Complete to match first side, reversing shapings.

SLEEVES (both alike)

Cast on 43 (45: 47: 49: 51: 53) sts using 3¼mm (US 3) needles.
Work in garter st for 3 rows, ending with a **RS** row.
Change to 3¾mm (US 5) needles.
Row 4 (WS): K1, *P1, K1, rep from * to end.
Row 5: As row 4.
Last 2 rows form moss st.
Cont in moss st, shaping sides by inc 1 st at each end of 6th and every foll 12th row

to 59 (71: 55: 67: 65: 77) sts, then on every
foll 14th (·: 14th: 14th: 14th: 14th) row until
there are 67 (·: 71: 75: 77: 81) sts.
Cont straight until sleeve measures 45 (46:
47: 48: 49: 50) cms, ending with a WS row.

Shape top

Cast off 3 (4: 4: 5: 5: 6) sts at beg of next
2 rows.
61 (63: 63: 65: 67: 69) sts.
Dec 1 st at each end of next 3 rows, then
on foll alt row, then on foll 4th row, then
on 3 foll 6th rows.
45 (47: 47: 49: 51: 53) sts.
Work 3 rows.
Dec 1 st at each end of next and 2 foll 4th
rows, then on every foll alt row to 37 sts,
then on foll 5 rows, ending with a WS row.
Cast off rem 27 sts.

MAKING UP

Pin the pieces out and steam gently without
allowing the iron to touch the yarn.
Join right shoulder seam using back stitch
or mattress stitch if preferred.

Neckband

With RS facing and using 3¼mm (US 3)
needles, pick up and knit 22 (22: 22: 26:
26: 26) sts down left side of neck, 21 (23:
23: 23: 23: 25) sts from front, 22 (22: 22:
26: 26: 26) sts up right side of neck, then
45 (47: 47: 49: 49: 51) sts from back.
110 (114: 114: 124: 124: 128) sts.
Beg with a K row, work in rev st st for 4 rows,
ending with a **RS** row.
Cast off knitwise (on **WS**).
Join left shoulder and neckband seam.
Join side seams. Join sleeve seams.
Insert sleeves into armholes.
Sew on buttons.

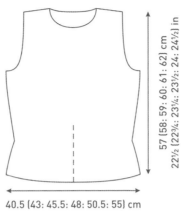

57 (58: 59: 60: 61: 62) cm
22½ (22¾: 23¼: 23½: 24: 24½) in

40.5 (43: 45.5: 48: 50.5: 55) cm
16 (17: 18: 19: 20: 21 ½) in

45 (46: 47: 48: 49: 50) cm
17¾ (18: 18½: 19: 19¼: 19¾) in

ALEXI

THE ULTIMATE CLASSIC CARDIGAN

Recommendation

Suitable for the knitter with a little experience
Please see pages 13 & 14 for photographs.

	XS	S	M	L	XL	XXL	
To fit	**81**	**86**	**91**	**97**	**102**	**109**	**cm**
bust	32	34	36	38	40	43	in

Rowan Pure Cashmere DK

11	12	13	13	14	15	x25gm

Photographed in Cork

Needles

1 pair 3mm (no 11) (US 2/3) needles
1 pair 3¼mm (no 10) (US 3) needles

Buttons – 9

Tension

27 sts and 37 rows to 10 cm measured over
stocking stitch using 3¼mm (US 3) needles.

BACK

Cast on 107 (115: 121: 127: 135: 147) sts
using 3mm (US 2/3) needles.
Work in garter st for 3 rows, ending with a **RS** row.
Row 4 (WS): P1, *K1, P1, rep from * to end.
Row 5: As row 4.
Last 2 rows form moss st.
Work in moss st for a further 9 rows, dec 1 st
at each end of 6th of these rows and ending with
a WS row. 105 (113: 119: 125: 133: 145) sts.
Change to 3¼mm (US 3) needles.
Beg with a K row, work in st st as folls:
Work 4 rows, ending with a WS row.
Next row (dec) (RS): K2, K2tog, K to last 4 sts,
K2tog tbl, K2.
Working all side seam decreases as set by last
row, dec 1 st at each end of 8th and 2 foll 8th
rows, then on 2 foll 6th rows.
93 (101: 107: 113: 121: 133) sts.
Work 13 rows, ending with a WS row.
Next row (inc) (RS): K3, M1, K to last 3 sts,
M1, K3.
Working all side seam increases as set by last
row, inc 1 st at each end of 10th and foll 10th
row, then on 5 foll 8th rows.
109 (117: 123: 129: 137: 149) sts.
Cont straight until back measures 37 (37: 38:
38: 38: 38) cm, ending with a WS row.

Shape armholes

Cast off 4 (5: 5: 6: 6: 7) sts at beg of next
2 rows. 101 (107: 113: 117: 125: 135) sts.
Dec 1 st at each end of next 3 (3: 5: 5: 7: 9)
rows, then on foll 3 (5: 5: 5: 6: 8) alt rows,
then on 2 foll 4th rows.
85 (87: 89: 93: 95: 97) sts.
Cont straight until armhole measures 18 (19:
19: 20: 21: 22) cm, ending with a WS row.

Shape shoulders and back neck

Cast off 7 (7: 8: 8: 8: 9) sts at beg of next 2
rows. 71 (73: 73: 77: 79: 79) sts.
Next row (RS): Cast off 7 (7: 8: 8: 8: 9) sts,
K until there are 12 (12: 11: 12: 13: 12) sts
on right needle and turn, leaving rem sts on
a holder.
Work each side of neck separately.
Cast off 4 sts at beg of next row.
Cast off rem 8 (8: 7: 8: 9: 8) sts.
With RS facing, rejoin yarn to rem sts, cast off
centre 33 (35: 35: 37: 37: 37) sts, K to end.
Complete to match first side, rev shapings.

POCKET LININGS (make 2)

Cast on 23 (23: 25: 25: 27: 27) sts using
3¼mm (US 3) needles.
Beg with a K row, work in st st for 22 rows,
ending with a WS row.
Break yarn and leave sts on a holder.

LEFT FRONT

Cast on 60 (64: 67: 70: 74: 80) sts using
3mm (US 2/3) needles.
Work in garter st for 3 rows, ending with
a **RS** row.
Row 4 (WS): P0 (0: 1: 0: 0: 0), *K1, P1, rep
from * to end.
Row 5: *P1, K1, rep from * to last 0 (0: 1: 0:
0: 0) st, P0 (0: 1: 0: 0: 0).
Last 2 rows form moss st.
Work in moss st for a further 9 rows, dec
1 st at beg of 6th of these rows and ending
with a WS row.
59 (63: 66: 69: 73: 79) sts.
Change to 3¼mm (US 3) needles.
Next row (RS): K to last 8 sts, moss st 8 sts.
Next row: Moss st 8 sts, P to end.
These 2 rows set the sts – front opening
edge 8 sts still in moss st with all other
sts now in st st.
Keeping sts correct as set and working all side
seam shaping in same way as given for back,
dec 1 st at beg of 3rd and 2 foll 8th rows.
56 (60: 63: 66: 70: 76) sts.
Work 1 row, ending with a WS row.

Place pocket

Next row (RS): K12 (15: 15: 17: 18: 23), slip
next 23 (23: 25: 25: 27: 27) sts onto a holder
and, in their place, K across 23 (23: 25: 25:
27: 27) sts of first pocket lining, K13 (14: 15:
16: 17: 18), moss st 8 sts.
Dec 1 st at beg of 6th and 2 foll 6th rows.
53 (57: 60: 63: 67: 73) sts.
Work 13 rows, ending with a WS row.
Inc 1 st at each end of next and 2 foll 10th
rows, then on 5 foll 8th rows.
61 (65: 68: 71: 75: 81) sts.
Cont straight until left front matches back to
beg of armhole shaping, ending with a WS row.

Shape armhole

Cast off 4 (5: 5: 6: 6: 7) sts at beg of next row.
57 (60: 63: 65: 69: 74) sts.
Work 1 row.

Dec 1 st at armhole edge of next 3 (3: 5: 5: 7: 9) rows, then on foll 3 (5: 5: 5: 6: 8) alt rows, then on 2 foll 4th rows.
49 (50: 51: 53: 54: 55) sts.
Cont straight until 21 (21: 21: 25: 25: 25) rows less have been worked than on back to beg of shoulder shaping, ending with a **RS** row.

Shape front neck

Next row (WS): Patt 15 (16: 16: 16: 16: 16) sts and slip these sts onto a holder, P to end.
34 (34: 35: 37: 38: 39) sts.
Dec 1 st at neck edge of next 7 rows, then on foll 4 alt rows, then on 1 (1: 1: 2: 2: 2) foll 4th rows.
22 (22: 23: 24: 25: 26) sts.
Work 1 row, ending with a WS row.

Shape shoulder

Cast off 7 (7: 8: 8: 8: 9) sts at beg of next and foll alt row.
Work 1 row.
Cast off rem 8 (8: 7: 8: 9: 8) sts.
Mark positions for 9 buttons along left front opening edge – first button level with row 9, top button just above neck shaping, and rem 7 buttons evenly spaced between.

RIGHT FRONT

Cast on 60 (64: 67: 70: 74: 80) sts using 3mm (US 2/3) needles.
Work in garter st for 3 rows, ending with a **RS** row.
Row 4 (WS): *P1, K1, rep from * to last 0 (0: 1: 0: 0: 0) st, P0 (0: 1: 0: 0: 0).
Row 5: P0 (0: 1: 0: 0: 0), *K1, P1, rep from * to end.
Last 2 rows form moss st.
Work in moss st for a further 3 rows, ending with a WS row.
Row 9 (buttonhole row) (RS): Moss st 3 sts, cast off 3 sts (to make a buttonhole – cast on 3 sts over these cast-off sts on next row), patt to end.
Making a further 7 buttonholes in this way to correspond with positions marked for buttons on left front and noting that no further reference will be made to buttonholes, cont as folls:
Work in moss st for a further 5 rows, dec 1 st at end of 2nd of these rows and ending with a WS row.
59 (63: 66: 69: 73: 79) sts.
Change to 3¼mm (US 3) needles.
Next row (RS): Moss st 8 sts, K to end.
Next row: P to last 8 sts, moss st 8 sts.
These 2 rows set the sts – front opening edge 8 sts still in moss st with all other sts now in st st.

Keeping sts correct as set and working all side seam shaping in same way as given for back, dec 1 st at end of 3rd and 2 foll 8th rows.
56 (60: 63: 66: 70: 76) sts.
Work 1 row, ending with a WS row.

Place pocket

Next row (RS): Moss st 8 sts, K13 (14: 15: 16: 17: 18), slip next 23 (23: 25: 25: 27: 27) sts onto a holder and, in their place, K across 23 (23: 25: 25: 27: 27) sts of second pocket lining, K12 (15: 15: 17: 18: 23).
Complete to match left front, reversing shapings and working first row of neck shaping as folls:

Shape front neck

Next row (RS): Patt 15 (16: 16: 16: 16: 16) sts and slip these sts onto a holder, K to end.
34 (34: 35: 37: 38: 39) sts.

SLEEVES (both alike)

Cast on 51 (53: 53: 55: 57: 59) sts using 3mm (US 2/3) needles.
Work in garter st for 3 rows, ending with a **RS** row.
Work in moss st as given for back for 11 rows, inc 1 st at each end of 10th of these rows and ending with a WS row.
53 (55: 55: 57: 59: 61) sts.
Change to 3¼mm (US 3) needles.
Beg with a K row and working all sleeve increases in same way as side seam increases, work in st st, shaping sides by inc 1 st at each end of 9th [7th: 7th: 7th: 7th: 7th] and every foll 10th (8th: 8th: 8th: 8th: 8th) row to 77 (59: 59: 67: 65: 73) sts, then on every foll 12th (10th: 10th: 10th: 10th: 10th) row until there are 79 (83: 83: 87: 89: 93) sts.
Cont straight until sleeve measures 44 (45: 45: 46: 47: 48) cm, ending with a WS row.

Shape top

Cast off 4 (5: 5: 6: 6: 7) sts at beg of next 2 rows.
71 (73: 73: 75: 77: 79) sts.
Dec 1 st at each end of next 3 rows, then on foll alt row, then on 8 foll 4th rows.
47 (49: 49: 51: 53: 55) sts.
Work 1 row.
Dec 1 st at each end of next and every foll alt row to 41 sts, then on foll 5 rows, ending with a WS row.
Cast off rem 31 sts.

MAKING UP

Pin the pieces out and steam gently without allowing the iron to touch the yarn.
Join both shoulder seams using back stitch or mattress stitch if preferred.

Neckband

With RS facing and using 3mm (US 2/3) needles, slip 15 (16: 16: 16: 16: 16) sts from right front holder onto right needle, rejoin yarn and pick up and knit 24 (24: 24: 27: 27: 27) sts up right side of neck, 41 (43: 43: 45: 45: 45) sts from back, and 24 (24: 24: 27: 27: 27) sts down left side of neck, then patt across 15 (16: 16: 16: 16: 16) sts on left front holder.
119 (123: 123: 131: 131: 131) sts.
Work in moss st as given for back for 7 rows, making 9th buttonhole in 4th of these rows and ending a WS row.
Work in garter st for 3 rows, ending with a **RS** row.
Cast off knitwise (on **WS**).

Pocket tops (both alike)

Slip 23 (23: 25: 25: 27: 27) sts from pocket holder onto 3mm (US 2/3) needles and rejoin yarn with RS facing.
Work in moss st as given for back for 6 rows, ending a WS row.
Work in garter st for 3 rows, ending with a **RS** row.
Cast off knitwise (on **WS**).
Join side seams. Join sleeve seams. Insert sleeves into armholes. Sew pocket linings in place on inside, then neatly sew down ends of pocket tops. Sew on buttons.

39.5 (42.5: 45: 47: 50: 54.5) cm
15½ (16¾: 17¾: 18½: 19½: 21½) in

55 (56: 57: 58: 59: 60) cm
21½ (22: 22½: 22¾: 23¼: 23½) in

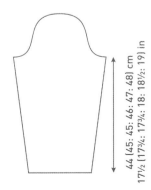

44 (45: 45: 46: 47: 48) cm
17½ (17¾: 17¾: 18: 18½: 19) in

Recommendation

Suitable for the knitter with a little experience
Please see pages 24 & 25 for photographs.

	XS	S	M	L	XL	XXL	
To fit	**81**	**86**	**91**	**97**	**102**	**109**	**cm**
bust	32	34	36	38	40	43	in

Rowan Big Wool

	5	5	6	6	7	7 x 100gm

Photographed in Black

Needles

1 pair 10mm (no 000) (US 15) needles
1 pair 12mm (US 17) needles

Buttons – 2

Tension

8 sts and 11 rows to 10 cm measured over
stocking stitch using 12mm (US 17) needles.

REBECCA

FITTED JACKET WITH GARTER STITCH PEPLUM

BODY

Peplum (worked in 2 pieces, beg at centre
back)
Cast on 12 (12: 13: 13: 14: 14) sts using
12mm (US 17) needles.
Row 1 (WS): Knit.
Place marker at end of this row to denote
upper edge.
Work in garter st for a further 27 (29: 31:
33: 35: 37) rows, ending with a **RS** row.
Shape side seam
Row 1: K9 (9: 10: 10: 11: 11), wrap next st
(by slipping next st from left needle to right
needle, taking yarn to opposite side of work
between needles and then slipping same st
back onto left needle – when working across
wrapped sts, work the wrapped st and the
wrapping loop tog as one st) and turn.
Row 2: Knit.
Row 3: K6 (6: 7: 7: 8: 8), wrap next st
and turn.
Rows 4 and 5: Knit.
Place marker at upper (marked) edge of
last row – this denotes base of side seam
for upper sections.
Row 6: Knit.
Row 7: As row 3.
Row 8: Knit.
Row 9: As row 1.
These 9 rows complete side seam shaping.
Work 16 (16: 18: 18: 20: 20) rows, ending
with a WS row.
Shape front hem edge
Next row (dec) (RS): K to last 3 sts, K2tog
tbl, K1.
Working all decreases as set by last row,
dec 1 st at end of 4th and foll 4 alt rows,
ending with a RS row. 6 (6: 7: 7: 8: 8) sts.
Next row (WS): K1, K2tog, K to end.
Working all RS row decreases as already set
and all WS row decreases as set by last row,
dec 1 st at shaped (lower) edge of next 3 (3:
4: 4: 5: 5) rows. 2 sts.
Next row: K2tog and fasten off.
With RS facing and using 12mm (US 17)
needles, pick up and knit 12 (12: 13: 13:
14: 14) sts along cast-on edge of section just
completed – this is centre back of peplum.
Work in garter st for 27 (29: 31: 33: 35: 37)
rows, ending with a WS row.

Shape side seam
Work the 9 side seam shaping rows as given
for first section.
Work 17 (17: 19: 19: 21: 21) rows, ending
with a WS row.
Shape front hem edge
Next row (dec) (RS): K1, K2tog, K to end.
Working all decreases as set by last row, dec
1 st at beg of 4th and foll 4 alt rows, ending
with a RS row.
6 (6: 7: 7: 8: 8) sts.
Next row (WS): K to last 3 sts, K2tog tbl, K1.
Working all RS row decreases as already set
and all WS row decreases as set by last row,
dec 1 st at shaped (lower) edge of next 3 (3:
4: 4: 5: 5) rows. 2 sts.
Next row: K2tog and fasten off but do **NOT**
break yarn.
Remove marker from upper edge of centre
back (cast-on and pick-up row) point of joined
peplum sections.
Upper sections
With RS facing and using 12mm (US 17)
needles, working along straight upper
(marked) edge of joined peplums, pick up
and knit 19 (20: 21: 22: 23: 24) sts from
last fasten-off point to first side seam marker,
remove marker from peplum and place
marker on last picked-up st – this denotes
right side seam, pick up and knit 29 (31: 33:
35: 37: 39) sts from centre section of peplum
to second side seam marker, then 19 (20:
21: 22: 23: 24) sts to fasten-off point of
first section of peplum, remove marker
from peplum and place marker on **first**
of this last set of picked-up sts – this
denotes left side seam.
67 (71: 75: 79: 83: 87) sts.
Next row (buttonhole row) (WS): K5 (6: 6:
6: 7: 7), P to last 5 (6: 6: 6: 7: 7) sts, K1
(2: 2: 2: 3: 3), yfwd, K2tog tbl (to make first
buttonhole), K2.
Next row: Knit.
Next row: K5 (6: 6: 6: 7: 7), P to last 5 (6: 6:
6: 7: 7) sts, K5 (6: 6: 6: 7: 7).
Last 2 rows set the sts - 5 (6: 6: 6: 7: 7) sts in
garter st at each end of row (for front bands)
with centre sts in st st.
Keeping sts correct as now set **throughout**,
cont as folls:

Work 7 rows, then rep the buttonhole row once more (2nd buttonhole made), ending with a WS row.

Shape side seams and front slopes

Next row (RS): K5 (6: 6: 6: 7: 7), K2tog (for front slope dec), *K to within 1 st of marked side seam st, M1, K3 (marked st is centre st of these 3 sts), M1, rep from * once more, K to last 7 (8: 8: 8: 9: 9) sts, K2tog tbl (for front slope dec), K5 (6: 6: 6: 7: 7).
69 (73: 77: 81: 85: 89) sts.
Work 5 (5: 5: 5: 7: 7) rows.
Next row: K5 (6: 6: 6: 7: 7), K2tog, K to last 7 (8: 8: 8: 9: 9) sts, K2tog tbl, K5 (6: 6: 6: 7: 7). 67 (71: 75: 79: 83: 87) sts.
Work 1 (3: 3: 3: 1: 1) rows.
Next row: *K to within 1 st of marked side seam st, M1, K3 (marked st is centre st of these 3 sts), M1, rep from * once more, K to end. 71 (75: 79: 83: 87: 91) sts.
Work 3 (3: 3: 3: 5: 5) rows.
Next row: K5 (6: 6: 6: 7: 7), K2tog, K to last 7 (8: 8: 8: 9: 9) sts, K2tog tbl, K5 (6: 6: 6: 7: 7). 69 (73: 77: 81: 85: 89) sts.
Work 1 row, ending with a WS row.

Divide for armholes

Next row (RS): K16 (17: 18: 19: 20: 21) and slip these sts onto a holder for right front, cast off 3 sts, K until there are 31 (33: 35: 37: 39: 41) sts on right needle and slip these sts onto another holder for back, cast off 3 sts, K to end.
Work on this set of 16 (17: 18: 19: 20: 21) sts only for left front as folls:
Dec 1 st at armhole edge of next 3 rows, then on foll 0 (0: 1: 1: 1: 1) alt row.
13 (14: 14: 15: 16: 17) sts.
Work 2 (2: 0: 0: 0: 0) rows, ending with a WS row.
Working front slope decreases as set, dec 1 st at front slope edge of next and foll 8th row.
11 (12: 12: 13: 14: 15) sts.
Cont straight until left front measures 18 (19: 19: 21: 21: 22) cm from underarm cast-off sts, ending with a WS row.

Shape shoulder

Cast off 3 (3: 3: 4: 4: 4) sts at beg of next row, then 3 (3: 3: 3: 3: 4) sts at beg of foll alt row.
Work in garter st on rem 5 (6: 6: 6: 7: 7) sts for a further 10 (12: 12: 12: 14: 14) rows (for back neck border extension), ending with a **RS** row.
Cast off knitwise (on **WS**).

Shape back

With **WS** facing, rejoin yarn to 31 (33: 35: 37: 39: 41) sts left on holder for back and cont as folls:

Dec 1 st at each end of next 3 rows, then on foll 0 (0: 1: 1: 1: 1) alt row.
25 (27: 27: 29: 31: 33) sts.
Cont straight until 2 rows less have been worked than on left front to start of shoulder shaping, ending with a WS row.

Shape back neck

Next row (RS): K8 (8: 8: 9: 9: 10) and turn, leaving rem sts on a holder.
Work each side of neck separately.
Dec 1 st at neck edge of next row, ending with a WS row.

Shape shoulder

Cast off 3 (3: 3: 4: 4: 4) sts at beg and dec 1 st at end of next row.
Work 1 row.
Cast off rem 3 (3: 3: 3: 3: 4) sts.
With RS facing, rejoin yarn to rem sts, cast off centre 9 (11: 11: 11: 13: 13) sts, K to end.
Complete to match first side, reversing shapings.

Shape right front

With **WS** facing, rejoin yarn to 16 (17: 18: 19: 20: 21) sts left on holder for right front and cont as folls:
Dec 1 st at armhole edge of next 3 rows, then on foll 0 (0: 1: 1: 1: 1) alt row.
13 (14: 14: 15: 16: 17) sts.
Complete to match left front, reversing shapings.

SLEEVES (both alike)

Cast on 18 (19: 20: 21: 22: 23) sts using 10mm (US 15) needles.
Work in garter st for 12 rows, ending with a **RS** row.
Change to 12mm (US 17) needles.
Beg with a K row, work in st st as folls:
Work 4 rows, ending with a WS row.
Next row (RS): K2, M1, K to last 2 sts, M1, K2.
Working all increases as set by last row, inc 1 st at each end of 14th and foll 12th row.
24 (25: 26: 27: 28: 29) sts.
Cont straight until sleeve measures 44 (45: 46: 47: 48: 49) cm, ending with a WS row.

Shape top

Cast off 2 sts at beg of next 2 rows.
20 (21: 22: 23: 24: 25) sts.
Dec 1 st at each end of next row, then on foll alt row, then on 1 (1: 1: 2: 2: 2) foll 4th rows.
14 (15: 16: 15: 16: 17) sts.
Work 1 row.
Dec 1 st at each end of next and foll 1 (1: 1: 0: 0: 1) alt row, then on foll row, ending with a WS row.
Cast off rem 8 (9: 10: 11: 12: 11) sts.

MAKING UP

Pin the pieces out and steam gently without allowing the iron to touch the yarn.
Join both shoulder seams using back stitch or mattress stitch if preferred. Join cast-off ends of back neck border extensions, then sew one edge to back neck.
Join sleeve seams. Insert sleeves into armholes.
Attach buttons to correspond with buttonholes.

41.5 (44: 46.5: 49: 51.5: 54) cm
16¼ (17¼: 18¼: 19¼: 20¼: 21¼) in

52 (55: 56: 58: 61: 62) cm
20½ (21¾: 22: 22¾: 24: 24½) in

44 (45: 46: 47: 48: 49) cm
17¼ (17¾: 18: 18½: 19: 19¼) in

MERRY

A VERY 'SLOPPY' JOE

Recommendation

Suitable for the knitter with a little experience
Please see pages 32 & 33 for photographs.

	XS	S	M	L	XL	XXL	
To fit	**81**	**86**	**91**	**97**	**102**	**109**	cm
bust	32	34	36	38	40	43	in

Rowan Kid Classic

10   11   12   12   13   14   x 50gm

Photographed in Plush

Needles

1 pair 3¾mm (no 9) (US 5) needles
1 pair 4½mm (no 7) (US 7) needles
3¾mm (no 9) (US 5) circular needle

Tension

21 sts and 27 rows to 10 cm measured over
stocking stitch using 4½mm (US 7) needles.

BACK

Cast on 146 (150: 154: 162: 166: 174) sts
using 4½mm (US 7) needles.
Row 1 (RS): K2, *P2, K2, rep from * to end.
Row 2: P2, *K2, P2, rep from * to end.
These 2 rows form rib.
Work in rib for a further 28 rows, dec 1 (0: 0:
1: 1: 0) st at each end of last row and ending
with a WS row.
144 (150: 154: 160: 164: 174) sts.
Beg with a K row, work in st st until back
measures 73 (74: 75: 76: 77: 78) cm,
ending with a WS row.

Shape shoulders and back neck

Cast off 9 (10: 10: 10: 11: 12) sts at beg of
next 4 (6: 6: 2: 6: 6) rows, then 10 (0: 0: 11:
0: 0) sts at beg of foll 2 (0: 0: 4: 0: 0) rows.
88 (90: 94: 96: 98: 102) sts.
Next row (RS): Cast off 10 (10: 11: 11: 11:
12) sts, K until there are 14 (14: 15: 15: 16:
17) sts on right needle and turn, leaving rem
sts on a holder.
Work each side of neck separately.
Cast off 4 sts at beg of next row.
Cast off rem 10 (10: 11: 11: 12: 13) sts.
With RS facing, rejoin yarn to rem sts, cast off
centre 40 (42: 42: 44: 44: 44) sts, K to end.
Complete to match first side, reversing
shapings.

FRONT

Work as given for back until 14 (14: 14: 16:
16: 16) rows less have been worked than on
back to beg of shoulder shaping, ending with
a WS row.

Shape front neck

Next row (RS): K60 (62: 64: 67: 69: 74)
and turn, leaving rem sts on a holder.
Work each side of neck separately.
Dec 1 st at neck edge of next 8 rows,
then on foll 2 (2: 2: 3: 3: 3) alt rows.
50 (52: 54: 56: 58: 63) sts.
Work 1 row, ending with a WS row.

Shape shoulder

Cast off 9 (10: 10: 10: 11: 12) sts at beg
of next and foll 1 (3: 2: 0: 3: 3) alt rows,
then 10 (0: 11: 11: 0: 0) sts at beg of foll
2 (0: 1: 3: 0: 0) alt rows **and at the same time**
dec 1 st at neck edge of next and foll 4th row.
Work 1 row.
Cast off rem 10 (10: 11: 11: 12: 13) sts.
With RS facing, rejoin yarn to rem sts,
cast off centre 24 (26: 26: 26: 26: 26) sts,
K to end.
Complete to match first side, reversing
shapings.

SLEEVES (both alike – worked from top downwards)

Join both shoulder seams using back stitch
or mattress stitch if preferred.
Place markers along side seam edges
22.5 (23: 23.5: 24: 24.5: 25) cm either side
of shoulder seams.
With RS facing and using 4½mm (US 7)
needles, pick up and knit 94 (96: 98:
100: 102: 104) sts evenly along row-end
edge between markers.
Beg with a **purl** row, now work in st st as folls:
Work 1 row.

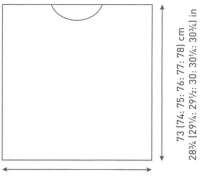

73 (74: 75: 76: 77: 78) cm
28¾ (29¼: 29½: 30: 30¼: 30¾) in

68.5 (71.5: 73.5: 76: 78: 83) cm
27 (28: 29: 30: 31: 32½) in

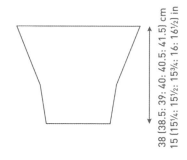

38 (38.5: 39: 40: 40.5: 41.5) cm
15 (15¼: 15½: 15¾: 16: 16½) in

Continued on next page...

OPAL

SHAWL
Cast on 1 st using 9mm (US 13) needles.
Row 1 (RS): Cast on 3 sts, cast off 2 sts, K to end. 2 sts.
Rows 2 to 8: As row 1. 9 sts.
Row 9: Cast on 3 sts, cast off 2 sts, K until there are 4 sts on right needle, yfwd, K2tog, K to end. 10 sts.
Rows 10 to 56: As row 9. 57 sts.

Row 57: Cast on 3 sts, cast off 2 sts, K until there are 4 sts on right needle, yfwd, K to end.
Row 58: As row 57.
Rows 59 and 60: As row 9. 63 sts.
Rows 61 to 80: As rows 57 to 60, 5 times. 93 sts.
Rows 81 to 104: As row 57.
Cast off all sts **very loosely**.

Recommendation
Suitable for the knitter with a little experience Please see pages 10, 19 & 34 for photographs.

Rowan Kidsilk Aura
    4   x 25gm
Photographed in Nearly Black, Vintage Orchard

Needles
1 pair 9mm (no 00) (US 13) needles

Tension
9 sts and 16 rows to 10 cm measured over garter stitch using 9mm (US 13) needles.

Finished size
Shawl measures approx 160 cm (63 in) wide and is 65 cm (25½ in) deep.

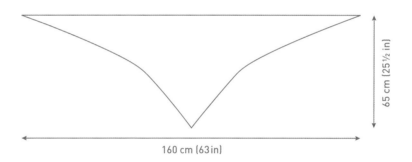

65 cm (25½ in)

160 cm (63 in)

Merry

Next row (dec) (RS): K2, K2tog, K to last 4 sts, K2tog tbl, K2.
Working all sleeve decreases as set by last row, dec 1 st at each end of 2nd and foll 8 (7: 6: 5: 4: 3) alt rows, then on 7 (8: 9: 10: 11: 12) foll 4th rows, then on foll 6th row.
58 (60: 62: 64: 66: 68) sts.
Work 1 row, ending with a WS row.
Change to 3¾mm (US 5) needles.
Next row (RS): K0 (1: 0: 1: 0: 1), P2, *K2, P2, rep from * to last 0 (1: 0: 1: 0: 1) st, K0 (1: 0: 1: 0: 1).

Next row: P0 (1: 0: 1: 0: 1), K2, *P2, K2, rep from * to last 0 (1: 0: 1: 0: 1) st, P0 (1: 0: 1: 0: 1). These 2 rows form rib.
Cont in rib, dec 1 st at each end of 3rd and 2 foll 6th rows, then on 2 foll 8th rows, then on foll 10th row. 46 (48: 50: 52: 54: 56) sts.
Work in rib for a further 9 rows, ending with a WS row.
Cast off in rib.

MAKING UP
Pin the pieces out and steam gently without allowing the iron to touch the yarn.

Neckband
With RS facing and using 3¾mm (US 5) circular needle, pick up and knit 24 (24: 24: 26: 26: 26) sts down left side of neck, 24 (26: 26: 26: 26: 26) sts from front, 24 (24: 24: 26: 26: 26) sts up right side of neck, then 48 (50: 50: 54: 54: 54) sts from back.
120 (124: 124: 132: 132: 132) sts.
Round 1 (RS): *K2, P2, rep from * to end.
Rep this round 5 times more.
Cast off in rib.
Join side and sleeve seams.

Recommendation

Suitable for the knitter with a little experience
Please see pages 28, 29 & 30 for photographs.

	XS	S	M	L	XL	XXL	
To fit	**81**	**86**	**91**	**97**	**102**	**109**	**cm**
bust	32	34	36	38	40	43	in

Rowan Felted Tweed

| | 9 | 10 | 10 | 11 | 11 | 12 | x 50gm |

Photographed in Ancient

Needles

1 pair 3¼ mm (no 10) (US 3) needles
1 pair 3¾mm (no 9) (US 5) needles
Cable needle

Buttons – 4

Tension

25 sts and 34 rows to 10 cm measured over
double moss stitch using 3¾mm (US 5)
needles.

SPECIAL ABBREVIATIONS

C8B = slip next 4 sts onto cn and leave at
back of work, K4, then K4 from cn; **C8F** = slip
next 4 sts onto cn and leave at front of work,
K4, then K4 from cn; **C10B** = slip next 5 sts
onto cn and leave at back of work, K5, then
K5 from cn; **C10F** = slip next 5 sts onto cn
and leave at front of work, K5, then K5 from
cn; **C12B** = slip next 6 sts onto cn and leave
at back of work, K6, then K6 from cn; **C12F**
= slip next 6 sts onto cn and leave at front of
work, K6, then K6 from cn; **C14B** = slip next
7 sts onto cn and leave at back of work, K7,
then K7 from cn; **C14F** = slip next 7 sts onto
cn and leave at front of work, K7, then K7
from cn.

SORREL

A-LINE JACKET FEATURING CABLES ON DOUBLE MOSS STITCH

BACK

Cast on 137 (143: 149: 155: 161: 171) sts
using 3¾mm (US 5) needles.
Row 1 (RS): K1 (0: 1: 0: 1: 0), (P1, K1) 9 (11:
11: 13: 13: 15) times, *P1, (K1, inc in next st)
4 times, K2, P1, (K1, inc in next st) 4 times,
K2, P1*, K1, (P1, K1) 7 (7: 8: 8: 9: 10) times,
rep from * to * once more, K1, (P1, K1) 7 (7:
8: 8: 9: 10) times, rep from * to * once more,
(K1, P1) 9 (11: 11: 13: 13: 15) times, K1 (0:
1: 0: 1: 0).
161 (167: 173: 179: 185: 195) sts.
Row 2: K1 (0: 1: 0: 1: 0), (P1, K1) 9 (11: 11:
13: 13: 15) times, *(K1, P14) twice, K1*, K1,
(P1, K1) 7 (7: 8: 8: 9: 10) times, rep from *
to * once more, K1, (P1, K1) 7 (7: 8: 8: 9: 10)
times, rep from * to * once more, (K1, P1) 9
(11: 11: 13: 13: 15) times, K1 (0: 1: 0: 1: 0).
Row 3: P1 (0: 1: 0: 1: 0), (K1, P1) 9 (11: 11:
13: 13: 15) times, *(P1, K14) twice, P1*, P1,
(K1, P1) 7 (7: 8: 8: 9: 10) times, rep from *
to * once more, P1, (K1, P1) 7 (7: 8: 8: 9: 10)
times, rep from * to * once more, (P1, K1) 9
(11: 11: 13: 13: 15) times, P1 (0: 1: 0: 1: 0).
Row 4: P1 (0: 1: 0: 1: 0), (K1, P1) 9 (11: 11:
13: 13: 15) times, *(K1, P14) twice, K1*, P1,
(K1, P1) 7 (7: 8: 8: 9: 10) times, rep from *
to * once more, P1, (K1, P1) 7 (7: 8: 8: 9: 10)
times, rep from * to * once more, (P1, K1) 9
(11: 11: 13: 13: 15) times, P1 (0: 1: 0: 1: 0).
These 4 rows set the sts – 3 cable panels with
double moss st between and at sides.
Keeping double moss st correct as now set,
cont as folls:
Row 5: Patt 19 (22: 23: 26: 27: 30) sts, *(P1,
K14) twice, P1*, patt 15 (15: 17: 17: 19:
21) sts, rep from * to * once more, patt 15
(15: 17: 17: 19: 21) sts, rep from * to * once
more, patt 19 (22: 23: 26: 27: 30) sts.
Row 6: Patt 19 (22: 23: 26: 27: 30) sts, *(K1,
P14) twice, K1*, patt 15 (15: 17: 17: 19:
21) sts, rep from * to * once more, patt 15
(15: 17: 17: 19: 21) sts, rep from * to * once
more, patt 19 (22: 23: 26: 27: 30) sts.
Rows 7 to 22: As rows 5 and 6, 8 times.
Row 23: Patt 19 (22: 23: 26: 27: 30) sts, *P1,
C14B, P1, C14F, P1*, patt 15 (15: 17: 17:
19: 21) sts, rep from * to * once more, patt
15 (15: 17: 17: 19: 21) sts, rep from * to *
once more, patt 19 (22: 23: 26: 27: 30) sts.

Row 24: As row 6.
Rows 5 to 24 form cable patt.
Cont as set for a further 38 rows, dec 1 st at
each end of 7th of these rows and ending with
a WS row.
159 (165: 171: 177: 183: 193) sts.
Row 63 (RS): Work 2 tog, patt 16 (19: 20: 23:
24: 27) sts, *P1, slip next 7 sts onto cn and
leave at back of work, K5, K2tog, then K2tog,
K5 from cn, P1, slip next 7 sts onto cn and
leave at front of work, K5, K2tog, then K2tog,
K5 from cn, P1*, patt 15 (15: 17: 17: 19:
21) sts, rep from * to * once more, patt 15
(15: 17: 17: 19: 21) sts, rep from * to * once
more, patt 16 (19: 20: 23: 24: 27) sts, work
2 tog. 145 (151: 157: 163: 169: 179) sts.
Row 64: Patt 17 (20: 21: 24: 25: 28) sts,
(K1, P12) twice, K1, patt 15 (15: 17: 17:
19: 21) sts, rep from * to * once more, patt
15 (15: 17: 17: 19: 21) sts, rep from * to *
once more, patt 17 (20: 21: 24: 25: 28) sts.
Row 65: Patt 17 (20: 21: 24: 25: 28) sts,
(P1, K12) twice, K1, patt 15 (15: 17: 17:
19: 21) sts, rep from * to * once more, patt
15 (15: 17: 17: 19: 21) sts, rep from * to *
once more, patt 17 (20: 21: 24: 25: 28) sts.
Rows 66 to 79: As rows 64 and 65, 7 times.
Row 80: As row 64.
Row 81: Patt 17 (20: 21: 24: 25: 28) sts, *P1,
C12B, P1, C12F, K1*, patt 15 (15: 17: 17:
19: 21) sts, rep from * to * once more, patt
15 (15: 17: 17: 19: 21) sts, rep from * to *
once more, patt 17 (20: 21: 24: 25: 28) sts.
Rows 82 to 97: As rows 64 and 65, 8 times.
Row 98: As row 64.
Row 99: Work 2 tog, patt 15 (18: 19: 22: 23:
26) sts, *P1, slip next 6 sts onto cn and leave
at back of work, K4, K2tog, then K2tog, K4
from cn, P1, slip next 6 sts onto cn and leave
at front of work, K4, K2tog, then K2tog, K4
from cn, P1*, patt 15 (15: 17: 17: 19: 21) sts,
rep from * to * once more, patt 15 (15: 17:
17: 19: 21) sts, rep from * to * once more,
patt 15 (18: 19: 22: 23: 26) sts, work 2 tog.
131 (137: 143: 149: 155: 165) sts.
Row 100: Patt 16 (19: 20: 23: 24: 27) sts,
(K1, P10) twice, K1, patt 15 (15: 17: 17:
19: 21) sts, rep from * to * once more, patt
15 (15: 17: 17: 19: 21) sts, rep from * to *
once more, patt 16 (19: 20: 23: 24: 27) sts.

Row 101: Patt 16 (19: 20: 23: 24: 27) sts, *(P1, K10) twice, K1*, patt 15 (15: 17: 17: 19: 21) sts, rep from * to * once more, patt 15 (15: 17: 17: 19: 21) sts, rep from * to * once more, patt 16 (19: 20: 23: 24: 27) sts.

Rows 102 to 113: As rows 100 and 101, 6 times.

Row 114: As row 100.

Row 115: Patt 16 (19: 20: 23: 24: 27) sts, *P1, C10B, P1, C10F, K1*, patt 15 (15: 17: 17: 19: 21) sts, rep from * to * once more, patt 15 (15: 17: 17: 19: 21) sts, rep from * to * once more, patt 16 (19: 20: 23: 24: 27) sts.

Rows 116 to 129: As rows 100 and 101, 7 times.

Row 130: As row 100.

Row 131: Patt 16 (19: 20: 23: 24: 27) sts, *P1, slip next 5 sts onto cn and leave at back of work, K3, K2tog, then K2tog, K3 from cn, P1, slip next 5 sts onto cn and leave at front of work, K3, K2tog, then K2tog, K3 from cn, P1*, patt 15 (15: 17: 17: 19: 21) sts, rep from * to * once more, patt 15 (15: 17: 17: 19: 21) sts, rep from * to * once more, patt 16 (19: 20: 23: 24: 27) sts.

119 (125: 131: 137: 143: 153) sts.

Row 132: Patt 16 (19: 20: 23: 24: 27) sts, *(K1, P8) twice, K1*, patt 15 (15: 17: 17: 19: 21) sts, rep from * to * once more, patt 15 (15: 17: 17: 19: 21) sts, rep from * to * once more, patt 16 (19: 20: 23: 24: 27) sts.

Row 133: Patt 16 (19: 20: 23: 24: 27) sts, *(P1, K8) twice, K1*, patt 15 (15: 17: 17: 19: 21) sts, rep from * to * once more, patt 15 (15: 17: 17: 19: 21) sts, rep from * to * once more, patt 16 (19: 20: 23: 24: 27) sts.

Rows 134 to 143: As rows 132 and 133, 5 times.

Row 144: As row 132.

Row 145: Patt 16 (19: 20: 23: 24: 27) sts, *P1, C8B, P1, C8F, K1*, patt 15 (15: 17: 17: 19: 21) sts, rep from * to * once more, patt 15 (15: 17: 17: 19: 21) sts, rep from * to * once more, patt 16 (19: 20: 23: 24: 27) sts.

Row 146: As row 132.

Last 14 rows form patt for rest of back.
Cont as now set (working 8 st cables on every 14th row) for a further 0 (0: 4: 4: 4: 4) rows, ending with a WS row.

Shape armholes

Keeping patt correct, cast off 5 (6: 6: 7: 7: 8) sts at beg of next 2 rows.
109 (113: 119: 123: 129: 137) sts.
Dec 1 st at each end of next 5 (5: 7: 7: 9: 11) rows, then on foll 3 (4: 4: 4: 4: 4) alt rows, then on foll 4th row. 91 (93: 95: 99: 101: 105) sts.
Cont straight until armhole measures 18 (19: 19: 20: 21: 22) cm, ending with a WS row.

Shape shoulders and back neck

Cast off 7 (7: 8: 8: 8: 9) sts at beg of next 2 rows.
77 (79: 79: 83: 85: 87) sts.

Next row (RS): Cast off 7 (7: 8: 8: 8: 9) sts, patt until there are 12 (12: 11: 12: 13: 12) sts on right needle and turn, leaving rem sts on a holder.
Work each side of neck separately.
Cast off 4 sts at beg of next row.
Cast off rem 8 (8: 7: 8: 9: 8) sts.
With RS facing, rejoin yarn to rem sts, cast off centre 39 (41: 41: 43: 43: 45) sts, patt to end. Complete to match first side, reversing shapings.

LEFT FRONT

Cast on 77 (80: 83: 86: 89: 94) sts using 3¾mm (US 5) needles.

Row 1 (RS): K1 (0: 1: 0: 1: 0), (P1, K1) 9 (11: 11: 13: 13: 15) times, P1, (K1, inc in next st) 4 times, K2, P1, (K1, inc in next st) 4 times, K2, (P1, K1) 18 (18: 19: 19: 20: 21) times.
85 (88: 91: 94: 97: 102) sts.

Row 2: (K1, P1) 7 times, K3, (P1, K1) 9 (9: 10: 10: 11: 12) times, (K1, P14) twice, K1, (K1, P1) 9 (11: 11: 13: 13: 15) times, K1 (0: 1: 0: 1: 0).

Row 3: P1 (0: 1: 0: 1: 0), (K1, P1) 9 (11: 11: 13: 13: 15) times, (P1, K14) twice, P2, (K1, P1) 9 (9: 10: 10: 11: 12) times, (P1, K1) 8 times.

Row 4: (K1, P1) 7 times, K2, P1, (K1, P1) 9 (9: 10: 10: 11: 12) times, (K1, P14) twice, K1, (P1, K1) 9 (11: 11: 13: 13: 15) times, P1 (0: 1: 0: 1: 0).

These 4 rows set the sts – cable panel with double moss st at both sides and front opening edge sts in moss st.
Keeping moss st and double moss st correct as now set, cont as folls:

Row 5: Patt 19 (22: 23: 26: 27: 30) sts, (P1, K14) twice, P1, patt 35 (35: 37: 37: 39: 41) sts.

Row 6: Patt 35 (35: 37: 37: 39: 41) sts, (K1, P14) twice, K1, patt 19 (22: 23: 26: 27: 30) sts.

Rows 7 to 22: As rows 5 and 6, 8 times.

Row 23: Patt 19 (22: 23: 26: 27: 30) sts, P1, C14B, P1, C14F, P1, patt 35 (35: 37: 37: 39: 41) sts.

Row 24: As row 6.
Rows 5 to 24 form cable patt.
Cont as set for a further 38 rows, dec 1 st at beg of 7th of these rows and ending with a WS row.
84 (87: 90: 93: 96: 101) sts.

Row 63 (RS): Work 2 tog, patt 16 (19: 20: 23: 24: 27) sts, P1, slip next 7 sts onto cn and leave at back of work, K5, K2tog, then K2tog, K5 from cn, P1, slip next 7 sts onto cn and leave at front of work, K5, K2tog, then K2tog, K5 from cn, P1, patt 35 (35: 37: 37: 39: 41) sts.
79 (82: 85: 88: 91: 96) sts.

Row 64: Patt 35 (35: 37: 37: 39: 41) sts, (K1, P12) twice, K1, patt 17 (20: 21: 24: 25: 28) sts.

Row 65: Patt 17 (20: 21: 24: 25: 28) sts, (P1, K12) twice, K1, patt 35 (35: 37: 37: 39: 41) sts.

Rows 66 to 79: As rows 64 and 65, 7 times.

Row 80: As row 64.

Row 81: Patt 17 (20: 21: 24: 25: 28) sts, P1, C12B, P1, C12F, K1, patt 35 (35: 37: 37: 39: 41) sts.

Rows 82 to 97: As rows 64 and 65, 8 times.

Row 98: As row 64.

Row 99: Work 2 tog, patt 15 (18: 19: 22: 23: 26) sts, P1, slip next 6 sts onto cn and leave at back of work, K4, K2tog, then K2tog, K4 from cn, P1, slip next 6 sts onto cn and leave at front of work, K4, K2tog, then K2tog, K4 from cn, P1, patt 35 (35: 37: 37: 39: 41) sts.
74 (77: 80: 83: 86: 91) sts.

Row 100: Patt 35 (35: 37: 37: 39: 41) sts, (K1, P10) twice, K1, patt 16 (19: 20: 23: 24: 27) sts.

Row 101: Patt 16 (19: 20: 23: 24: 27) sts, (P1, K10) twice, K1, patt 35 (35: 37: 37: 39: 41) sts.

Rows 102 to 113: As rows 100 and 101, 6 times.

Row 114: As row 100.

Row 115: Patt 16 (19: 20: 23: 24: 27) sts, P1, C10B, P1, C10F, K1, patt 35 (35: 37: 37: 39: 41) sts.

Rows 116 to 129: As rows 100 and 101, 7 times.

Row 130: As row 100.

Row 131: Patt 16 (19: 20: 23: 24: 27) sts, P1, slip next 5 sts onto cn and leave at back of work, K3, K2tog, then K2tog, K3 from cn, P1, slip next 5 sts onto cn and leave at front of work, K3, K2tog, then K2tog, K3 from cn, P1, patt 35 (35: 37: 37: 39: 41) sts.
70 (73: 76: 79: 82: 87) sts.

Row 132: Patt 35 (35: 37: 37: 39: 41) sts, (K1, P8) twice, K1, patt 16 (19: 20: 23: 24: 27) sts.

Row 133: Patt 16 (19: 20: 23: 24: 27) sts, (P1, K8) twice, K1, patt 35 (35: 37: 37: 39: 41) sts.

Rows 134 to 143: As rows 132 and 133, 5 times.

Row 144: As row 132.

Row 145: Patt 16 (19: 20: 23: 24: 27) sts, P1, C8B, P1, C8F, K1, patt 35 (35: 37: 37: 39: 41) sts.

Row 146: As row 132.

Last 14 rows form patt for rest of left front. Cont as now set (working 8 st cables on every 14th row) for a further 0 (0: 4: 4: 4: 4) rows, ending with a WS row.

Shape armhole

Keeping patt correct, cast off 5 (6: 6: 7: 7: 8) sts at beg of next row.

65 (67: 70: 72: 75: 79) sts.

Work 1 row.

Dec 1 st at armhole edge of next 5 (5: 7: 7: 9: 11) rows, then on foll 3 (4: 4: 4: 4: 4) alt rows, then on foll 4th row.

56 (57: 58: 60: 61: 63) sts.

Cont straight until 20 (20: 20: 22: 22: 22) rows less have been worked than on back to beg of shoulder shaping, ending with a WS row.

Shape neck

Next row (RS): Patt 34 (34: 35: 37: 38: 39) sts and turn, leaving rem 22 (23: 23: 23: 23: 24) sts on a holder.

Keeping patt correct, dec 1 st at neck edge of next 8 rows, then on foll 3 (3: 3: 4: 4: 4) alt rows, then on foll 4th row.

22 (22: 23: 24: 25: 26) sts.

Work 1 row, ending with a WS row.

Shape shoulder

Cast off 7 (7: 8: 8: 8: 9) sts at beg of next and foll alt row.

Work 1 row.

Cast off rem 8 (8: 7: 8: 9: 8) sts.

Mark positions for 4 buttons along left front opening edge – first to come 10 cm below armhole shaping, last to come level with neck shaping, and rem 2 buttons evenly spaced between.

RIGHT FRONT

Cast on 77 (80: 83: 86: 89: 94) sts using 3¾mm (US 5) needles.

Row 1 (RS): (K1, P1) 18 (18: 19: 19: 20: 21) times, K2, P1, (K1, inc in next st) 4 times, K2, P1, (K1, inc in next st) 4 times, (K1, P1) 9 (11: 11: 13: 13: 15) times, K1 (0: 1: 0: 1: 0).

85 (88: 91: 94: 97: 102) sts.

Row 2: K1 (0: 1: 0: 1: 0), (P1, K1) 9 (11: 11: 13: 13: 15) times, (K1, P14) twice, K1, (K1, P1) 9 (9: 10: 10: 11: 12) times, K3, (P1, K1) 7 times.

Row 3: (K1, P1) 8 times, (P1, K1) 9 (9: 10: 10: 11: 12) times, P2, (K14, P1) twice, (P1, K1) 9 (11: 11: 13: 13: 15) times, P1 (0: 1: 0: 1: 0).

Row 4: P1 (0: 1: 0: 1: 0), (K1, P1) 9 (11: 11: 13: 13: 15) times, (K1, P14) twice, K1, (P1, K1) 9 (9: 10: 10: 11: 12) times, P1, K2, (P1, K1) 7 times.

These 4 rows set the sts – cable panel with double moss st at both sides and front opening edge sts in moss st.

Keeping moss st and double moss st correct as now set, cont as folls:

Row 5: Patt 35 (35: 37: 37: 39: 41) sts, (P1, K14) twice, P1, patt 19 (22: 23: 26: 27: 30) sts.

Row 6: Patt 19 (22: 23: 26: 27: 30) sts, (K1, P14) twice, K1, patt 35 (35: 37: 37: 39: 41) sts.

Rows 7 to 22: As rows 5 and 6, 8 times.

Row 23: Patt 35 (35: 37: 37: 39: 41) sts, P1, C14B, P1, C14F, P1, patt 19 (22: 23: 26: 27: 30) sts.

Row 24: As row 6.

Rows 5 to 24 form cable patt.

Cont as set for a further 38 rows, dec 1 st at end of 7th of these rows and ending with a WS row.

84 (87: 90: 93: 96: 101) sts.

Complete to match left front, reversing shapings, making buttonholes to correspond with positions marked for buttons and working first row of neck shaping as folls:

Buttonhole row (RS): Patt 6 sts, cast off 4 sts (to make a buttonhole – cast on 4 sts over these cast-off sts on next row), patt to end.

Shape neck

Next row (RS): Patt 6 sts, cast off 4 sts (to make 4th buttonhole – cast on 4 sts over these cast-off sts on next row), patt until there are 12 (13: 13: 13: 13: 14) sts on right needle after cast-off and slip these sts onto a holder, patt to end. 34 (34: 35: 37: 38: 39) sts.

SLEEVES (both alike)

Cuff (knitted sideways)

Cast on 44 sts using 3¾mm (US 5) needles.

Row 1 (RS): K15, P1, K12, P1, K15.

Row 2: K5, P10, K1, P12, K1, P10, K5.

Rep these 2 rows 3 (0: 0: 1: 2: 3) times more.

Now work in patt as folls:

Row 1 (RS): K5, C10B, P1, C8B, K4, P1, C10F, K5.

Row 2 and every foll alt row: K5, P10, K1, P12, K1, P10, K5.

Row 3: K15, P1, K12, P1, K15.

Rows 5 and 7: K15, P1, K12, P1, K15.

Row 9: K15, P1, K4, C8F, P1, K15.

Rows 11, 13 and 15: As row 3.

Row 16: As row 2.

These 16 rows form patt.

Rep last 16 rows 5 (6: 6: 6: 6: 6) times more, then rows 1 and 2 again.

Next row (RS): K15, P1, K12, P1, K15.

Next row: K5, P10, K1, P12, K1, P10, K5.

Rep these 2 rows 3 (0: 0: 2: 3: 4) times more, ending with a WS row.

Cast off all 44 sts but do **NOT** break yarn.

Main sleeve

With RS facing and 3¾mm (US 5) needles, pick up and knit 81 (85: 85: 89: 91: 95) sts evenly along row-end edge of cuff.

Row 1 (WS): K1, *P1, K1, rep from * to end.

Rows 2 and 3: P1, *K1, P1, rep from * to end.

Row 4: As row 1.

These 4 rows form double moss st.

Cont in double moss st, shaping sides by dec 1 st at each end of 16th and 2 foll 20th rows. 75 (79: 79: 83: 85: 89) sts.

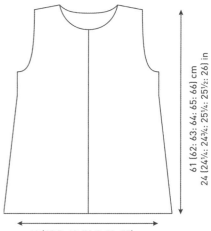

43 (45.5: 48: 50.5: 53: 57) cm
17 (18: 19: 20: 21: 22½) in

61 (62: 63: 64: 65: 66) cm
24 (24¼: 24¾: 25¼: 25½: 26) in

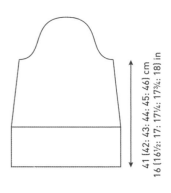

41 (42: 43: 44: 45: 46) cm
16 (16½: 17: 17¼: 17¾: 18) in

Continued on next page...

Recommendation
Suitable for the novice knitter
Please see pages 12, 15 & 51 for photographs.

One size

Rowan Pure Cashmere DK
   2   x 25gm
Photographed in Blush, Greige & Marina

Needles
1 pair 2¾mm (no 12) (US 2) needles
1 pair 3¼mm (no 10) (US 3) needles

Tension
27 sts and 37 rows to 10 cm measured over
stocking stitch using 3¼mm (US 3) needles.

CHERRY
CHEEKY CASHMERE BERET

BERET
Cast on 127 sts using 2¾mm (US 2) needles.
Work in garter st for 3 rows, ending with a
RS row.
Row 4 (WS): K1, *P1, K1, rep from * to end.
Rows 5 to 12: As row 4.
Change to 3¼mm (US 3) needles.
Beg with a K row, now work in st st as folls:
Row 1 (RS): *K2, inc in next st, (K1, inc in next
st) twice, rep from * to last st, K1. 181 sts.
Work 5 rows.
Row 7: *K9, inc in next st, rep from * to last
st, K1. 199 sts.
Work 5 rows.
Row 13: *K10, inc in next st, rep from * to
last st, K1. 217 sts.
Work 17 rows, ending with a WS row.
Row 31: *K22, K2tog, rep from * to last st,
K1. 208 sts.
Work 3 rows.
Row 35: *K21, K2tog, rep from * to last st,
K1. 199 sts.
Work 3 rows.
Row 39: *K20, K2tog, rep from * to last st,
K1. 190 sts.

Work 1 row.
Row 41: *K19, K2tog, rep from * to last st,
K1. 181 sts.
Work 1 row.
Row 43: *K18, K2tog, rep from * to last st,
K1. 172 sts.
Work 1 row.
Row 45: *K17, K2tog, rep from * to last st,
K1. 163 sts.
Work 1 row.
Row 47: *K16, K2tog, rep from * to last st,
K1. 154 sts.
Work 1 row.
Row 49: *K15, K2tog, rep from * to last st,
K1. 145 sts.
Work 1 row.
Cont in this way, dec 9 sts on next and every
foll alt row, until the foll row has been worked:
Row 77: *K1, K2tog, rep from * to last st, K1.
Break yarn and thread through rem 19 sts.
Pull up tight and fasten off securely.

MAKING UP
Join back seam, preferably using mattress
stitch.

Sorrel - Continued from previous page...

Cont straight until sleeve measures 29 (30:
31: 32: 33: 34) cm **from pick-up row**, ending
with a WS row.
Shape top
Keeping patt correct, cast off 5 (6: 6: 7: 7: 8)
sts at beg of next 2 rows.
65 (67: 67: 69: 71: 73) sts.
Dec 1 st at each end of next 3 rows, then on
foll alt row, then on 7 foll 4th rows.
43 (45: 45: 47: 49: 51) sts.
Work 3 rows.
Dec 1 st at each end of next and every foll alt
row to 39 sts, then on foll 5 rows, ending with
a WS row. Cast off rem 29 sts.

MAKING UP
Pin the pieces out and steam gently without
allowing the iron to touch the yarn.
Join both shoulder seams using back stitch
or mattress stitch if preferred.

Neckband
With RS facing and using 3¼mm (US 3)
needles, slip sts from right front holder onto
right needle, rejoin yarn and pick up and knit
24 (24: 24: 26: 26: 26) sts up right side of
neck, 39 (41: 41: 43: 43: 45) sts from back,
and 24 (24: 24: 26: 26: 26) sts down left side
of neck, then patt across 22 (23: 23: 23: 23:
24) sts on left front holder. 131 (135: 135:

141: 141: 145) sts (including the 4 sts of the
5th buttonhole to be cast on on next row).
Next row (WS): Patt first 16 sts as set by left
front, work in double moss st as set by rem
sts of left front holder sts to last 16 sts, patt
to end (remembering to cast on 4 sts over
buttonhole sts).
Cont as now set for a further 6 rows, ending
with a WS row.
Cast off in patt.
Join side seams. Join sleeve seams. Insert
sleeves into armholes. Fold garter st section
around lower edge of cuff to inside and neatly
slip stitch in place. Sew on buttons.

Recommendation

Suitable for the knitter with a little experience
Please see pages 45, 48 & 49 for photographs.

	XS	S	M	L	XL	XXL	
To fit	**81**	**86**	**91**	**97**	**102**	**109**	**cm**
bust	32	34	36	38	40	43	in

Rowan Kid Classic

	8	8	9	9	10	10	x 50gm

Photographed in Nightly

Needles

1 pair 4½mm (no 7) (US 7) needles

Tension

21 sts and 27 rows to 10 cm measured over
stocking stitch using 4½mm (US 7) needles.

BACK

Cast on 96 (100: 106: 110: 116: 126) sts
quite loosely using 4½mm (US 7) needles.
Row 1 (RS): K4 (4: 5: 5: 6: 6), wrap next
st (by slipping next st from left needle to
right needle, taking yarn to opposite side
of work between needles and then slipping
same st back onto left needle – when
working across wrapped sts, work the
wrapped st and the wrapping loop tog
as one st) and turn.
Row 2: Purl.
Row 3: K8 (8: 10: 10: 12: 12), wrap next st
and turn.
Row 4: Purl.
Row 5: K13 (14: 16: 17: 19: 20), wrap next st
and turn.
Row 6: Purl.
Row 7: K18 (20: 22: 24: 26: 28), wrap next st
and turn.
Row 8: Purl.
Row 9: K26 (28: 31: 33: 36: 38), wrap next st
and turn.
Row 10: Purl.
Row 11: Knit across all sts.
Row 12: P4 (4: 5: 5: 6: 6), wrap next st and
turn.
Row 13: Knit.
Row 14: P8 (8: 10: 10: 12: 12), wrap next st
and turn.
Row 15: Knit.
Row 16: P13 (14: 16: 17: 19: 20), wrap next
st and turn.
Row 17: Knit.
Row 18: P18 (20: 22: 24: 26: 28), wrap next
st and turn.
Row 19: Knit.
Row 20: P26 (28: 31: 33: 36: 38), wrap next
st and turn.
Row 21: Knit.
Row 22: Purl across **all** sts.
This completes hem shaping.
Beg with a K row, work in st st as folls:
Work 4 rows, ending with a WS row.
Next row (dec) (RS): K3, K2tog, K to last
5 sts, K2tog tbl, K3.
Working all side seam decreases as set by
last row, dec 1 st at each end of 10th and
3 foll 10th rows.
86 (90: 96: 100: 106: 116) sts.

Work 45 (45: 47: 47: 47: 47) rows, ending
with a WS row. (Back should measure 34 (34:
35: 35: 35: 35) cm at centre.)
Shape armholes
Cast off 3 (4: 4: 5: 5: 6) sts at beg of next
2 rows. 80 (82: 88: 90: 96: 104) sts.
Dec 1 st at each end of next 5 (5: 7: 7: 9: 11)
rows, then on foll 2 alt rows, then on foll 4th
row. 64 (66: 68: 70: 72: 76) sts.
Cont straight until armhole measures 17 (18:
18: 19: 20: 21) cm, ending with a WS row.
Shape back neck
Next row (RS): K17 (17: 18: 18: 19: 20)
and turn, leaving rem sts on a holder.
Work each side of neck separately.
Dec 1 st at neck edge of next 2 rows.
15 (15: 16: 16: 17: 18) sts.
Work 1 row, ending with a WS row.
Shape shoulder
Cast off 7 (7: 7: 7: 8: 8) sts at beg and
dec 1 st at end of next row.
Work 1 row.
Cast off rem 7 (7: 8: 8: 8: 9) sts.
With RS facing, rejoin yarn to rem sts, cast off
centre 30 (32: 32: 34: 34: 36) sts, K to end.
Complete to match first side, rev shapings.

LEFT FRONT

Cast on 82 (84: 87: 89: 92: 97) sts **quite
loosely** using 4½mm (US 7) needles.
Row 1 (RS): Knit.
Row 2: P6, wrap next st and turn.
Row 3: Knit.
Row 4: P10, wrap next st and turn.
Row 5: Knit.
Row 6: P14, wrap next st and turn.
Row 7: Knit.
Row 8: P18, wrap next st and turn.
Row 9: Knit.
Row 10: P23 (24: 24: 24: 24: 24), wrap next
st and turn.
Row 11: K to last 5 sts, K2tog tbl, K3.
Row 12: P27 (29: 29: 29: 29: 29), wrap next
st and turn.
Row 13: Knit.
Row 14: P33 (35: 35: 35: 35: 35), wrap next
st and turn.
Row 15: Knit.
Row 16: P39 (41: 41: 41: 41: 42), wrap next
st and turn.

Row 17: As row 11.
Row 18: P44 (46: 46: 47: 47: 49), wrap next st and turn.
Row 19: Knit.
Row 20: P50 (52: 53: 55: 55: 57), wrap next st and turn.
Row 21: Knit.
Row 22: P56 (57: 60: 62: 62: 65), wrap next st and turn.
Row 23: As row 11.
Row 24: P63 (65: 68: 70: 71: 74), wrap next st and turn.
Row 25: Knit.
Row 26: P71 (73: 76: 78: 80: 84), wrap next st and turn.
Row 27: Knit.
Row 28: Purl across **all** sts.
79 (81: 84: 86: 89: 94) sts.
This completes hem shaping.
Working all side seam decreases as set by back, all front slope decreases as set by rows 11, 17 and 23 and beg with a K row, now work in st st as folls:
Dec 1 st at front slope edge of next and 16 foll 6th rows **and at same time** dec 1 st at side seam edge of 15th and 4 foll 10th rows.
57 (59: 62: 64: 67: 72) sts.
Work 3 (3: 5: 5: 5: 5) rows, ending with a WS row.

Shape armhole
Cast off 3 (4: 4: 5: 5: 6) sts at beg and dec 0 (0: 1: 1: 1: 1) st at end of next row.
54 (55: 57: 58: 61: 65) sts.
Work 1 row.
Dec 1 st at armhole edge of next 5 (5: 7: 7: 9: 11) rows, then on foll 2 alt rows, then on foll 4th row **and at same time** dec 1 st at front slope edge of 3rd (next: 5th: 5th: 5th: 5th) and 0 (2: 0: 1: 1: 2) foll 6th rows, then on 1 (0: 1: 0: 0: 0) foll 8th row.
44 (44: 45: 46: 47: 48) sts.
Dec 1 st at front slope edge **only** on 6th (8th: 6th: 2nd: 2nd: 4th) and 0 (0: 0: 0: 0: 1) foll 6th row, then on 0 (0: 0: 1: 1: 0) foll 8th row, then on foll 10th row.
42 (42: 43: 43: 44: 45) sts.
Cont straight until left front matches back to start of shoulder shaping, ending with a WS row.

Shape shoulder
Cast off 7 (7: 7: 7: 8: 8) sts at beg of next row, then 7 (7: 8: 8: 8: 9) sts at beg of foll alt row.
Cont in st st on these 28 sts only for a further 10.5 (11: 11: 11.5: 11.5: 12) cm, ending with a RS row.

Next row (WS): P19, wrap next st and turn.
Next row: Knit.
Next row: P9, wrap next st and turn.
Next row: Knit.
Cast off purlwise (on **WS**).

RIGHT FRONT
Cast on 82 (84: 87: 89: 92: 97) sts **quite loosely** using 4½mm (US 7) needles.
Row 1 (RS): K6, wrap next st and turn.
Row 2: Purl.
Row 3: K10, wrap next st and turn.
Row 4: Purl.
Row 5: K14, wrap next st and turn.
Row 6: Purl.
Row 7: K18, wrap next st and turn.
Row 8: Purl.
Row 9: K23 (24: 24: 24: 24: 24), wrap next st and turn.
Row 10: Purl.
Row 11: K3, K2tog, K until there are 27 (29: 29: 29: 29: 29) sts on right needle, wrap next st and turn.
Complete to match left front, reversing shapings.

SLEEVES (both alike)
Cast on 40 (42: 44: 46: 48: 50) sts using 4½mm (US 7) needles.
Row 1 (RS): K1 (0: 1: 0: 1: 0), P2, *K2, P2, rep from * to last 1 (0: 1: 0: 1: 0) st, K1 (0: 1: 0: 1: 0).
Row 2: P1 (0: 1: 0: 1: 0), K2, *P2, K2, rep from * to last 1 (0: 1: 0: 1: 0) st, P1 (0: 1: 0: 1: 0).
These 2 rows form rib.
Cont in rib for a further 18 rows, inc 1 st at each end of 11th of these rows and ending with a WS row. 42 (44: 46: 48: 50: 52) sts.
Beg with a K row, now work in st st as folls:
Work 0 (0: 2: 0: 0: 0) rows.
Next row (inc) (RS): K3, M1, K to last 3 sts, M1, K3.
Working all increases as set by last row, inc 1 st at each end of 8th (8th: 10th: 8th: 8th: 8th) and every foll 10th (8th: 10th: 8th: 10th: 8th) row to 62 (56: 64: 54: 72: 62) sts, then on every foll · (10th: 12th: 10th: -: 10th) row until there are - (66: 66: 70: -: 76) sts.
Cont straight until sleeve measures 45 (46: 47: 48: 49: 50) cm, ending with a WS row.

Shape top
Cast off 3 (4: 4: 5: 5: 6) sts at beg of next 2 rows. 56 (58: 58: 60: 62: 64) sts.
Dec 1 st at each end of next 3 rows, then on foll alt row, then on 4 foll 4th rows.
40 (42: 42: 44: 46: 48) sts.

Work 3 rows.
Dec 1 st at each end of next and every foll alt row to 36 sts, then on foll 5 rows, ending with a WS row.
Cast off rem 26 sts.

MAKING UP
Pin the pieces out and steam gently without allowing the iron to touch the yarn.
Join both shoulder seams using back stitch or mattress stitch if preferred. Join cast-off ends of back neck border extensions, then sew one edge to back neck. Join side seams. Join sleeve seams. Insert sleeves into armholes.

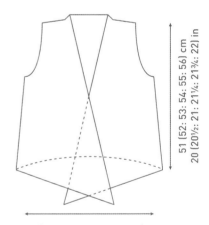

51 (52: 53: 54: 55: 56) cm
20 (20½: 21: 21¼: 21¾: 22) in

40.5 (43: 45.5: 48: 50.5: 55.5) cm
16 (17: 18: 19: 20: 22) in

45 (46: 47: 48: 49: 50) cm
17¾ (18: 18½: 19: 19¼: 19¾) in

FLEUR
CLASSIC SWEATER WITH LACY RUFFLE TRIM

Recommendation
Suitable for the knitter with a little experience
Please see pages 42 & 43 for photographs.

	XS	S	M	L	XL	XXL	
To fit	**81**	**86**	**91**	**97**	**102**	**109**	**cm**
bust	32	34	36	38	40	43	in

Yarn A Cashsoft 4 ply

	4	5	5	6	6	7	x 50gm

Yarn B Kidsilk Haze

	1	1	1	1	1	1	x 25gm

Photographed in Deep trimmed with Pearl

Needles
1 pair 2¼mm (no 13) (US 1) needles
1 pair 2¾mm (no 12) (US 2) needles
1 pair 3mm (no 11) (US 2/3) needles
1 pair 3¼mm (no 10) (US 3) needles
2.25mm (no 13) (US B1) crochet hook

Buttons – 1

Beads – 174 (174: 174: 192: 192: 192) small
glass beads

Tension
28 sts and 38 rows to 10 cm measured over
stocking stitch using 3mm (US 2/3) needles.

BACK
Cast on 103 (109: 117: 123: 131: 141) sts
using 2¾mm (US 2) needles and yarn A.
Work in garter st for 3 rows, ending with
a **RS** row.
Row 4 (WS): P1, *K1, P1, rep from * to end.
Row 5: As row 4.
Last 2 rows form moss st.
Work in moss st for a further 7 rows,
dec 1 st at each end of 4th of these rows
and ending with a WS row.
101 (107: 115: 121: 129: 139) sts.
Change to 3mm (US 2/3) needles.
Beg with a K row, work in st st as folls:
Work 2 rows, ending with a WS row.
Next row (dec) (RS): K2, K2tog, K to last
4 sts, K2tog tbl, K2.
Working all side seam decreases as set by
last row, dec 1 st at each end of 6th and 2 foll
6th rows. 93 (99: 107: 113: 121: 131) sts.
Work 15 rows, ending with a WS row.
Next row (inc) (RS): K3, M1, K to last 3 sts,
M1, K3.
Working all side seam increases as set by last
row, inc 1 st at each end of 12th and foll 12th
row, then on 4 foll 10th rows.
107 (113: 121: 127: 135: 145) sts.
Cont straight until back measures 32 (32: 33:
33: 33: 33) cm, ending with a WS row.
Shape armholes
Cast off 4 (5: 5: 6: 6: 7) sts at beg of next
2 rows. 99 (103: 111: 115: 123: 131) sts.
Dec 1 st at each end of next 7 (7: 9: 9: 11:
13) rows, then on foll 2 (3: 4: 4: 5: 5) alt
rows, then on foll 4th row.
79 (81: 83: 87: 89: 93) sts.
Cont straight until armhole measures 10 (11:
11: 11: 12: 13) cm, ending with a WS row.
Divide for back opening
Next row (RS): K38 (39: 40: 42: 43: 45)
and turn, leaving rem sts on a holder.
Work each side of neck separately.
Dec 1 st at opening edge of next 2 rows,
then on foll 1 (1: 1: 2: 2: 2) alt rows.
35 (36: 37: 38: 39: 41) sts.
Work 5 rows, ending with a WS row.
Inc 1 st at opening edge of next and foll 1 (1:
1: 2: 2: 2) alt rows, then on 2 foll 4th rows.
39 (40: 41: 43: 44: 46) sts.
Work 4 rows, ending with a **RS** row.

Shape back neck and shoulder
Cast off 18 (19: 19: 20: 20: 21) sts at beg
of next row.
21 (21: 22: 23: 24: 25) sts.
Cast off 6 (6: 6: 7: 7: 7) sts at beg of next and
foll alt row **and at same time** dec 1 st at neck
edge of next 3 rows.
Work 1 row.
Cast off rem 6 (6: 7: 6: 7: 8) sts.
With RS facing, rejoin yarn to rem sts, cast
off centre 3 sts, K to end.
Complete to match first side, rev shapings.

FRONT
Work as given for back until 12 (12: 12: 16:
16: 16) rows less have been worked than on
back to beg of armhole shaping, ending with
a WS row.
Mark ruffle placement
Place marker on centre st of last row.
Now working this marked centre st as
a **purl** st on RS rows and a **knit** st on WS
rows **throughout**, cont as given for back until
26 (26: 26: 30: 30: 30) rows less have been
worked than on back to beg of shoulder
shaping, ending with a WS row.
Shape front neck
Next row (RS): K30 (30: 31: 33: 34: 35)
and turn, leaving rem sts on a holder.
Work each side of neck separately.
Dec 1 st at neck edge of next 6 rows, then
on foll 5 alt rows, then on 1 (1: 1: 2: 2: 2)
foll 4th rows.
18 (18: 19: 20: 21: 22) sts.
Work 5 rows, ending with a WS row.
Shape shoulder
Cast off 6 (6: 6: 7: 7: 7) sts at beg of next
and foll alt row.
Work 1 row.
Cast off rem 6 (6: 7: 6: 7: 8) sts.
With RS facing, rejoin yarn to rem sts, cast off
centre 19 (21: 21: 21: 21: 23) sts, K to end.
Complete to match first side, rev shapings.

SLEEVES (both alike)
Cast on 73 (77: 77: 81: 83: 87) sts using
2¾mm (US 2) needles and yarn B **DOUBLE**.
Break off yarn B and join in yarn A.
Work in garter st for 3 rows, ending
with a **RS** row.

Work in moss st as given for back for 9 rows, inc 1 st at each end of 6th of these rows and ending with a WS row.
75 (79: 79: 83: 85: 89) sts.
Change to 3mm (US 2/3) needles.
Beg with a K row, work in st st as folls:
Work 2 rows, ending with a WS row.

Shape top
Cast off 4 (5: 5: 6: 6: 7) sts at beg of next 2 rows. 67 (69: 69: 71: 73: 75) sts.
Dec 1 st at each end of next 3 rows, then on foll alt row, then on 7 foll 4th rows.
45 (47: 47: 49: 51: 53) sts.
Work 1 row.
Dec 1 st at each end of next and every foll alt row to 39 sts, then on foll 7 rows, ending with a WS row.
Cast off rem 25 sts.

MAKING UP
Pin the pieces out and steam gently without allowing the iron to touch the yarn.
Using 2.25mm (US B1) crochet hook and yarn A, work a row of double crochet neatly around back opening, beg and ending at top of opening.
Fasten off.
Join both shoulder seams using back stitch or mattress stitch if preferred.

Neckband
With RS facing, using 2¼mm (US 1) needles and yarn A, beg and ending at back opening edges, pick up and knit 23 (24: 24: 25: 25: 26) sts from left side of back neck, 26 (26: 26: 29: 29: 29) sts down left side of front neck, 19 (21: 21: 21: 21: 23) sts from front, 26 (26: 26: 29: 29: 29) sts up right side of front neck, then 23 (24: 24: 25: 25: 26) sts from right side of back neck.
117 (121: 121: 129: 129: 133) sts.
Work in moss st as given for back for 5 rows, ending a WS row.
Cast off in moss st.

Long ruffle
Thread 110 (110: 110: 128: 128: 128) beads onto yarn B.
Using 3¼mm (US 3) needles and yarn B, work beaded cast-on as folls: cast on 1 st (onto left needle), *slide a bead up close to st on left needle, insert right needle point into st on left needle as if to K this st, take yarn round needle, draw loop through and place this loop onto left needle – 1 beaded st cast on, cast on 1 st (without a bead), rep from * until there are 221 (221: 221: 257: 257: 257) sts on left needle.

Row 1 (RS): K1, *K2, lift 2nd st on right needle over first st and off right needle, rep from * to end.
111 (111: 111: 129: 129: 129) sts.
Row 2: Knit.
Row 3: K1, (K1, yfwd, K1) all into next st, (K1 wrapping yarn twice round needle) 5 times, *(K1, yfwd, K1, yfwd, K1) all into next st, (K1 wrapping yarn twice round needle) 5 times, rep from * to last 2 sts, (K1, yfwd, K1) all into next st, K1.
Row 4: K4, slip next 5 sts from left needle to right needle dropping extra loops, slip same 5 sts back onto left needle and P these 5 sts tog, *K5, slip next 5 sts from left needle to right needle dropping extra loops, slip same 5 sts back onto left needle and P these 5 sts tog, rep from * to last 4 sts, K4.
Beg with a K row, now work in st st as folls:
Work 6 rows, ending with a WS row.
Row 11 (RS): K1, (K2tog) to end.
56 (56: 56: 65: 65: 65) sts.
Work 6 rows, ending with a RS row.
Row 18 (WS): P0 (0: 0: 1: 1: 1), (P2tog) to end.
Cast off rem 28 (28: 28: 33: 33: 33) sts **very loosely**.
Neatly sew cast-off edge of ruffle to ruffle placement line on front as in photograph.

Lower neck ruffle
Thread 38 beads onto yarn B.
Using 3¼mm (US 3) needles and yarn B, work beaded cast-on as given for long ruffle until there are 77 sts on left needle.
Now work rows 1 to 17 as given for long ruffle, noting that there will be 39 sts after row 1, and 20 sts after row 11.
Row 18 (WS): (P2tog) to end.
Cast off rem 10 sts **very loosely**.
Neatly sew cast-off edge of ruffle to centre front neck edge just below neckband pick-up row as in photograph.

Upper neck ruffle
Thread 26 beads onto yarn B.
Using 3¼mm (US 3) needles and yarn B, work beaded cast-on as given for long ruffle until there are 53 sts on left needle.
Now work rows 1 to 17 as given for long ruffle, noting that there will be 27 sts after row 1, and 14 sts after row 11.
Row 18 (WS): (P2tog) to end.
Cast off rem 7 sts **very loosely**.
Neatly sew cast-off edge of ruffle to centre front neck edge along neckband pick-up row as in photograph.

Join side seams. Join sleeve seams.
Insert sleeves into armholes.
Make a button loop and attach button to fasten ends of neckband at centre back neck.

49 (50: 51: 52: 53: 54) cm
19¼ (19¾: 20: 20½: 21: 21¼) in

38 (40.5: 43: 45.5: 48: 52) cm
15 (16: 17: 18: 19: 20½) in

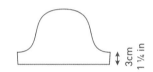

3cm
1¼ in

Recommendation

Suitable for the knitter with a little experience
Please see pages 46 & 47 for photographs.

	XS-S	M-L	XL-XXL	
To fit	**81-86**	**91-97**	**102-109**	**cm**
bust	32-34	36-38	40-43	in

Rowan Big Wool

	5	6	7	x	100gm

Photographed in Commodore

Needles

1 pair 8mm (no 0) (US 11) needles
1 pair 10mm (no 000) (US 15) needles
Cable needle

Buttons · 3

Tension

9½ sts and 15 rows to 10 cm measured over
moss stitch using 10mm (US 15) needles.

VALENTINE
MOSS STITCH CABLED CAPE WITH NEAT COLLAR

CAPE (knitted in one piece)
Cast on 139 (147: 155) sts using 10mm (US
15) needles.
Row 1 (RS): K1 (0: 1), (P1, K1) 7 (8: 8)
times, *(K1, inc in next st) twice, K2, P1,
(K1, inc in next st) twice, K2*, K1, (P1, K1)
10 (11: 12) times, rep from * to * once
more, K1, (P1, K1) 7 (8: 9) times, rep from
* to * once more, K1, (P1, K1) 10 (11: 12)
times, rep from * to * once more, (K1, P1)
7 (8: 8) times, K1 (0: 1).
155 (163: 171) sts.
Row 2: K1 (0: 1), (P1, K1) 7 (8: 8) times,
P8, K1, P8, K1, (P1, K1) 10 (11: 12)
times, P8, K1, P8, K1, (P1, K1) 7 (8: 9)
times, P8, K1, P8, K1, (P1, K1) 10 (11: 12)
times, P8, K1, P8, (K1, P1) 7 (8: 8) times,
K1 (0: 1).
Row 3: K1 (0: 1), (P1, K1) 7 (8: 8)
times, K8, P1, K9, (P1, K1) 10 (11: 12)
times, K8, P1, K9, (P1, K1) 7 (8: 9) times,
K8, P1, K9, (P1, K1) 10 (11: 12) times, K8,
P1, K8, (K1, P1) 7 (8: 8) times, K1 (0: 1).
Last 2 rows set the sts – 4 cable panels
with moss st between and at sides.
Cont as set for a further 7 (9: 9) rows,
ending with a WS row.
Next row (RS): Patt 15 (16: 17) sts,
*slip next 4 sts onto cn and leave at
back of work, K4, then K4 from cn, P1,
slip next 4 sts onto cn and leave at front
of work, K4, then K4 from cn*, patt
21 (23: 25) sts, rep from * to * once more,
patt 15 (17: 19) sts, rep from * to * once
more, patt 21 (23: 25) sts, rep from * to *
once more, patt 15 (16: 17) sts.
Work 7 (7: 9) rows, ending with a WS row.
Shape shoulder darts
Counting in from both ends of last row, place
markers on 43rd (45th: 47th) sts in from both
ends of row.
Row 1 (RS): *Patt to within 1 st of marked st,
work 3 tog (marked st is centre st of these
3 sts), rep from * once more, patt to end.
151 (159: 167) sts.
Work 1 row.
Row 3 (RS): Patt 15 (16: 17) sts, *slip next
4 sts onto cn and leave at back of work, K2,
K2tog, then K2tog, K2 from cn, P1, slip next
4 sts onto cn and leave at front of work, K2,

K2tog, then K2tog, K2 from cn*, patt 19
(21: 23) sts, rep from * to * once more,
patt 15 (17: 19) sts, rep from * to * once
more, patt 19 (21: 23) sts, rep from * to *
once more, patt 15 (16: 17) sts.
135 (143: 151) sts.
Noting that there are now only 6 sts in
each cable (instead of 8 sts), cont as folls:
Work 5 rows.
Row 9: Patt 2 sts, work 2 tog, yrn (to make
first buttonhole), *patt to within 1 st of
marked st, work 3 tog (marked st is centre
st of these 3 sts), rep from * once more,
patt to end.
131 (139: 147) sts.
Making a further 2 buttonholes in this way
on 12th and foll 12th row and noting that no
further reference will be made to buttonholes,
cont as folls:
Work 1 row.
Row 11: Patt 15 (16: 17) sts, *slip next
3 sts onto cn and leave at back of work,
K3, then K3 from cn, P1, slip next 3 sts
onto cn and leave at front of work, K3,
then K3 from cn*, patt 17 (19: 21) sts,
rep from * to * once more, patt
15 (17: 19) sts, rep from * to * once more,
patt 17 (19: 21) sts, rep from * to * once
more, patt 15 (16: 17) sts.
Work 3 rows.
Row 15: As row 1.
127 (135: 143) sts.
Work 3 rows.
Row 19: Patt 15 (16: 17) sts, *slip next
3 sts onto cn and leave at back of work,
K1, K2tog, then K2tog, K1 from cn, P1,
slip next 3 sts onto cn and leave at front
of work, K1, K2tog, then K2tog, K1 from
cn*, patt 7 (8: 9) sts, work 3 tog (marked
st is centre st of these 3 sts), patt
7 (8: 9) sts, rep from * to * once more,
patt 15 (17: 19) sts, rep from * to * once
more, patt 7 (8: 9) sts, work 3 tog
(marked st is centre st of these 3 sts),
patt 7 (8: 9) sts, rep from * to * once
more, patt 15 (16: 17) sts.
107 (115: 123) sts.
Noting that there are now only 4 sts in each
cable (instead of 6 sts), cont as folls:
Work 3 rows.

Row 23: As row 1.
103 (111: 119) sts.
Work 1 row.
Row 25: Patt 15 (16: 17) sts, *slip next
2 sts onto cn and leave at back of work,
K2, then K2 from cn, P1, slip next 2 sts
onto cn and leave at front of work, K2,
then K2 from cn*, patt 11 (13: 6) sts,
(work 3 tog, patt 6 sts) 0 (0: 1) times,
rep from * to * once more, patt
15 (17: 19) sts, rep from * to * once more,
patt 11 (13: 6) sts, (work 3 tog, patt 6 sts)
0 (0: 1) times, rep from * to * once more,
patt 15 (16: 17) sts. 103 (111: 115) sts.
Work 1 row.
Row 27: As row 1.
99 (107: 111) sts.
Work 1 row.
Row 29: (Patt to within 1 st of marked st,
work 3 tog - marked st is centre st of these
3 sts) 0 (2: 2) times, patt to end.
99 (103: 107) sts.
Remove markers.
Work 1 row.
Row 31: Patt 13 (14: 15) sts, work 2 tog tbl,
*slip next 2 sts onto cn and leave at back of
work, K2tog, then K2tog from cn, P1, slip
next 2 sts onto cn and leave at front of work,
K2tog, then K2tog from cn*, patt 3 sts, work
3 tog, patt 3 sts, rep from * to * once more,
work 2 tog tbl, patt 11 (13: 15) sts, work 2
tog, rep from * to * once more, patt 3 sts,
work 3 tog, patt 3 sts, rep from * to * once
more, work 2 tog, patt 13 (14: 15) sts.
75 (79: 83) sts.
Noting that there are now only 2 sts in each
cable (instead of 4 sts), cont as folls:
Work 1 row.
Row 33: Patt 14 (13: 14) sts, (work 2 tog tbl)
0 (1: 1) times, K2, P1, K2, patt 2 sts, work
3 tog, patt 2 sts, K2, P1, K2, (work 2 tog tbl)
0 (1: 1) times, patt 13 (11: 13) sts, (work
2 tog) 0 (1: 1) times, K2, P1, K2, patt 2 sts,
work 3 tog, patt 2 sts, K2, P1, K2, (work 2
tog) 0 (1: 1) times, patt 14 (13: 14) sts.
71 (71: 75) sts.
Change to 8mm (US 11) needles.
Work 1 row.
Row 35: Patt 12 (12: 13) sts, work 2 tog tbl,
K2tog, P1, K2tog, patt 1 st, work 3 tog and
mark resulting st with a coloured thread, patt
1 st, K2tog, P1, K2tog, work 2 tog tbl, patt 9
(9: 11) sts, work 2 tog, K2tog, P1, K2tog, patt
1 st, work 3 tog and mark resulting st with a
coloured thread, patt 1 st, K2tog, P1, K2tog,
work 2 tog, patt 12 (12: 13) sts.
55 (55: 59) sts.

Row 36: Cast off 4 sts, patt until there are
9 (9: 10) sts on right needle, cast off next
29 (29: 31) sts, patt to end.
Row 37: Cast off 4 sts, patt until there are
9 (9: 10) sts on right needle, now work across
cast-off sts as folls: pick up and knit 4 sts to
marked st, 1 st from marked st, 19 sts to
next marked st, 1 st from this marked st,
then 4 sts to next set of sts on left needle,
patt 9 (9: 10) sts.
47 (47: 49) sts.
Shape collar
Now working in moss st across all sts as set
by first and last 9 (9: 10) sts of previous row,
cont as folls:
Row 1 (RS of collar, WS of body): Patt to end.
Row 2: *Patt to within 1 st of marked st, work
3 tog (marked st is centre st of these 3 sts),
rep from * once more, patt to end.
43 (43: 45) sts.
Rep last 2 rows once more.
39 (39: 41) sts.
Work 9 (10: 11) rows.
**Next row: Patt 12 sts, wrap next st (by
slipping next st from left needle to right
needle, taking yarn to opposite side of work
between needles and then slipping same st
back onto left needle) and turn.
Next row: Patt 12 sts.
Next row: Patt 8 sts, wrap next st and turn.
Next row: Patt 8 sts.
Next row: Patt 4 sts, wrap next st and turn.
Next row: Patt 4 sts.**
Work 1 row across all sts.
Rep from ** to ** once more.
Cast off all sts in moss st.

MAKING UP
Press using a warm iron over a damp cloth.
Sew on buttons.

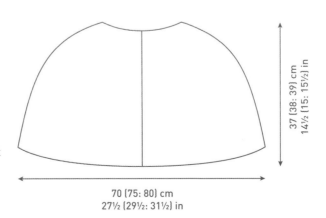

37 (38: 39) cm
14½ (15: 15½) in

70 (75: 80) cm
27½ (29½: 31½) in

LIVI

A DELIGHTFULLY PRETTY SWEATER

Recommendation

Suitable for the more experienced knitter
Please see pages 35 & 36 for photographs.

	XS	S	M	L	XL	XXL	
To fit	**81**	**86**	**91**	**97**	**102**	**109**	**cm**
bust	32	34	36	38	40	43	in

Rowan Pure Cashmere DK

7	8	8	9	9	10	x 25gm

Photographed in Blush

Needles

1 pair 3mm (no 11) (US 2/3) needles
1 pair 3¼mm (no 10) (US 3) needles

Tension

27 sts and 37 rows to 10 cm measured over stocking stitch using 3¼mm (US 3) needles.

Special abbreviations

cluster 2 = yrn, P2, lift the yrn over these 2 sts and off right needle.

Pattern note: The number of sts varies whilst working the border patt. All st counts given presume there are 9 sts in every patt rep **at all times** and do **not**, therefore, include the sts made whilst working patt. Take care when working patt row 7 that each K4tog tbl and K4tog is worked correctly.

BACK

Cast on 170 (186: 196: 208: 218: 240) sts using 3¼mm (US 3) needles.
Row 1 (WS): K1, *sl 1, K1, psso, rep from * to last st, K1.
86 (94: 99: 105: 110: 121) sts.
Now work in border patt as folls:
Row 1 (RS): K3 (7: 5: 8: 6: 7), *yfwd, K8, yfwd, K1, rep from * to last 2 (6: 4: 7: 5: 6) sts, K to end.
Row 2: K3 (7: 5: 8: 6: 7), *K1, P8, K2, rep from * to last 2 (6: 4: 7: 5: 6) sts, K to end.
Row 3: K3 (7: 5: 8: 6: 7), *K1, yfwd, K8, yfwd, K2, rep from * to last 2 (6: 4: 7: 5: 6) sts, K to end.
Row 4: K3 (7: 5: 8: 6: 7), *K2, P8, K3, rep from * to last 2 (6: 4: 7: 5: 6) sts, K to end.
Row 5: K3 (7: 5: 8: 6: 7), *K2, yfwd, K8, yfwd, K3, rep from * to last 2 (6: 4: 7: 5: 6) sts, K to end.
Row 6: K3 (7: 5: 8: 6: 7), *K3, P8, K4, rep from * to last 2 (6: 4: 7: 5: 6) sts, K to end.
Row 7: K3 (7: 5: 8: 6: 7), *K3, K4tog tbl, K4tog, K4, rep from * to last 2 (6: 4: 7: 5: 6) sts, K to end.
Row 8: Knit.
These 8 rows form border patt.
Cont in border patt, dec 1 st at each end of 13th and foll 20th row.
82 (90: 95: 101: 106: 117) sts.
Work a further 4 rows, ending after patt row 5 and with a RS row.
Row 46 (WS): Purl.
Row 47: K1 (5: 3: 6: 4: 5), *K4, K3tog tbl, K3tog, K5, rep from * to last 0 (4: 2: 5: 3: 4) sts, K0 (4: 2: 5: 3: 4).
100 (108: 115: 121: 128: 141) sts.
Row 48: Purl, dec 0 (0: 1: 1: 0: 1) st at centre of row.
100 (108: 114: 120: 128: 140) sts.
These 48 rows complete border.
Next row (dec) (RS): K2, K2tog, K to last 4 sts, K2tog tbl, K2.
98 (106: 112: 118: 126: 138) sts.
Working all side seam decreases as set by last row (and noting that the "K2tog" and "K2tog tbl" are **NOT** shown on chart) cont as folls:
Next row: Purl.

Beg and ending rows as indicated and repeating the 12 row patt rep throughout, now work in patt from chart for body as folls:
Dec 1 st at each end of 5th and 3 foll 6th rows. 90 (98: 104: 110: 118: 130) sts.
Work 23 rows, ending with a WS row.
Next row (inc) (RS): K3, M1, K to last 3 sts, M1, K3.
Working all side seam increases as set by last row, inc 1 st at each end of 6th and 8 foll 6th rows, taking inc sts into patt.
110 (118: 124: 130: 138: 150) sts.
Cont straight until back measures approx 40 (40: 41: 41: 41: 41) cm, ending after patt row 4 or 10 and with a WS row.
Shape raglan armholes
Keeping patt correct, cast off 6 sts at beg of next 2 rows.
98 (106: 112: 118: 126: 138) sts.
Sizes XS and S only
Next row (RS): K3, patt to last 3 sts, K3.
Next row: P3, patt to last 3 sts, P3.
Next row: K2, K2tog, K to last 4 sts, K2tog tbl, K2.
Next row: P3, patt to last 3 sts, P3.
Rep last 4 rows 3 (2: ·: ·: ·: ·) times more.
90 (100: ·: ·: ·: ·) sts.
Sizes XL and XXL only
Next row: K2, K2tog, K to last 4 sts, K2tog tbl, K2.
Next row: P2, P2tog tbl, patt to last 4 sts, P2tog, P2.
Rep last 2 rows · (·: ·: ·: 1: 3) times more.
· (·: ·: ·: 118: 122) sts.
All sizes
Next row: K2, K2tog, K to last 4 sts, K2tog tbl, K2.
Next row: P3, patt to last 3 sts, P3.
Rep last 2 rows 11 (15: 21: 23: 23: 23) times more, ending with a WS row.
Cast off rem 66 (68: 68: 70: 70: 74) sts.

FRONT

Work as given for back until 80 (82: 82: 86: 86: 90) sts rem in raglan armhole shaping. Work 1 row, ending with a WS row.
Shape front neck
Next row (RS): K2, K2tog, patt 10 (10: 10: 12: 12: 12) sts and turn, leaving rem sts on a holder.

Work each side of neck separately.
Dec 1 st at neck edge of next 6 rows, then
on foll 0 (0: 0: 1: 1: 1) alt row **and at same
time** dec 1 st at raglan armhole edge of
2nd and foll 2 (2: 2: 3: 3: 3) alt rows. 4 sts.
Next row (WS): P4.
Next row: K1, sl 1, K2tog, psso.
Next row: P2.
Next row: K2tog and fasten off.
With RS facing, rejoin yarn to rem sts, cast off
centre 52 (54: 54: 54: 54: 58) sts, patt to last
4 sts, K2tog tbl, K2.
Complete to match first side, reversing
shapings.

SLEEVES (both alike)
Cast on 116 (124: 124: 126: 134: 142) sts
using 3¼mm (US 3) needles.
Row 1 (WS): K1, *sl 1, K1, psso, rep from * to
last st, K1. 59 (63: 63: 64: 68: 72) sts.
Now work in border patt as folls:
Row 1 (RS): K3 (5: 5: 1: 3: 5), *yfwd, K8,
yfwd, K1, rep from * to last 2 (4: 4: 0: 2: 4)
sts, K2 (4: 4: 0: 2: 4).
Row 2: K3 (5: 5: 1: 3: 5), *K1, P8, K2, rep
from * to last 2 (4: 4: 0: 2: 4) sts, K2 (4: 4: 0:
2: 4).
Row 3: K3 (5: 5: 1: 3: 5), *K1, yfwd, K8, yfwd,
K2, rep from * to last 2 (4: 4: 0: 2: 4) sts, K2
(4: 4: 0: 2: 4).
Row 4: K3 (5: 5: 1: 3: 5), *K2, P8, K3, rep
from * to last 2 (4: 4: 0: 2: 4) sts, K2 (4: 4: 0:
2: 4).
Row 5: K3 (5: 5: 1: 3: 5), *K2, yfwd, K8, yfwd,
K3, rep from * to last 2 (4: 4: 0: 2: 4) sts, K2
(4: 4: 0: 2: 4).
Row 6: K3 (5: 5: 1: 3: 5), *K3, P8, K4, rep
from * to last 2 (4: 4: 0: 2: 4) sts, K2 (4: 4: 0:
2: 4).
Row 7: K3 (5: 5: 1: 3: 5), *K3, K4tog tbl,
K4tog, K4, rep from * to last 2 (4: 4: 0: 2: 4)
sts, K2 (4: 4: 0: 2: 4).
Row 8: Knit.
These 8 rows form border patt.
Cont in border patt, inc 1 st at each end
of next row.
61 (65: 65: 66: 70: 74) sts.
Work a further 4 rows, ending after patt
row 5 and with a **RS** row.
Row 14 (WS): Purl.
Row 15: Inc in first st, K3 (5: 5: 1: 3: 5), *K4,
K3tog tbl, K3tog, K5, rep from * to last 3 (5:
5: 1: 3: 5) sts, K2 (4: 4: 0: 2: 4), inc in last st.
75 (79: 79: 82: 86: 90) sts.
Row 16: Purl, dec 1 (1: 1: 0: 0: 0) st at centre
of row. 74 (78: 78: 82: 86: 90) sts.
These 16 rows complete border.

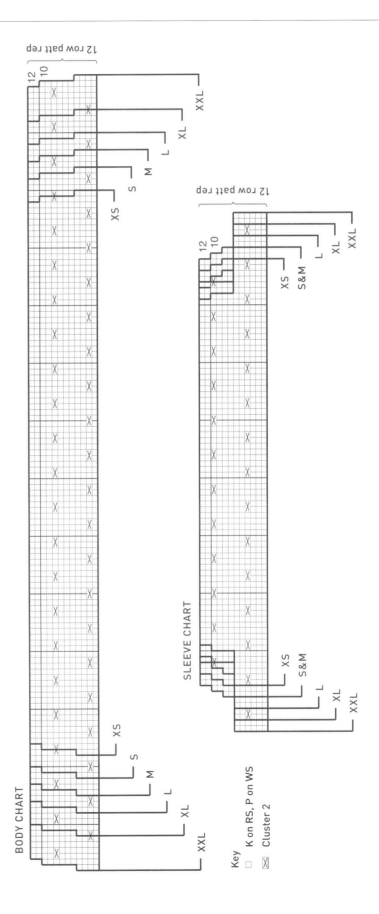

Beg and ending rows as indicated and
repeating the 12 row patt rep throughout,
now work in patt from chart for sleeve as folls:
Work 6 rows, ending with a WS row.

Shape raglan

Keeping patt correct, cast off 6 sts at beg
of next 2 rows.
62 (66: 66: 70: 74: 78) sts.
Working all raglan decreases in same way
as raglan armhole decreases, dec 1 st at
each end of 3rd (3rd: 3rd: next: next: next)
and 2 (0: 0: 0: 0: 0) foll 6th rows, then on
foll 0 (0: 0: 1: 3: 5) alt rows, then on every
foll 4th row until 46 sts rem, ending with
a **RS** row.

Left sleeve only

Work 2 rows.
Cast off 15 sts at beg of next and foll alt row,
ending with a WS row, **and at same time** dec
1 st at beg of 2nd row.

Right sleeve only

Work 1 row.
Cast off 15 sts at beg of next and foll
alt row **and at same time** dec 1 st at
end of 3rd row.
Work 1 row, ending with a WS row.

Both sleeves

Cast off rem 15 sts.

MAKING UP

Pin the pieces out and steam gently without
allowing the iron to touch the yarn.
Join both front and right back raglan seams
using back stitch or mattress stitch if
preferred.

Neckband

With RS facing and using 3mm (US 2/3)
needles, pick up and knit 44 sts from
top of left sleeve placing marker between
centre 2 sts, place a second marker on
right needle, pick up and knit 9 (9: 9:
11: 11: 11) sts down left side of neck,
52 (54: 54: 54: 54: 58) sts from front,
and 9 (9: 9: 11: 11: 11) sts up right side
of neck, place a 3rd marker on right
needle, pick up and knit 44 sts from top
of right sleeve placing 4th marker between
centre 2 sts, place a 5th marker on right
needle, then pick up and knit 64 (66: 66:
68: 68: 72) sts from back.
222 (226: 226: 232: 232: 240) sts.

Row 1 (WS): Knit.

Row 2: K2, K2tog, *K to within 4 sts of
marker, K2tog tbl, K4 (marker is between
centre 2 sts of these 4 sts), K2tog, rep from
* 4 times more, K to last 4 sts, K2tog tbl, K2.
210 (214: 214: 220: 220: 228) sts.

Rep last 2 rows 4 times more, ending with
a **RS** row.
Cast off rem 162 (166: 166: 172: 172: 180)
sts knitwise (on **WS**).
Join left back raglan and neckband seam.
Join side and sleeve seams.

40.5 (43.5: 46: 48: 51: 55.5) cm
16 (17: 18: 19: 20: 21½) in

59.5 (60.5: 61.5: 63.5: 64.5: 65.5) cm
23½ (23¾: 24¼: 25: 25½: 25¾) in

6 cm
2½ in

DIVINE
CLOSE FITTING SHRUG WITH OVERSIZED CABLES

Recommendation
Suitable for the knitter with a little experience
Please see pages 8 & 16 for photographs.

	XS	S	M	L	XL	XXL	
To fit	**81**	**86**	**91**	**97**	**102**	**109**	cm
bust	32	34	36	38	40	43	in

Rowan Big Wool

3	3	4	4	5	5 x 100gm

Photographed in Lichen & Glum

Needles
1 pair 10mm (no 000) (US 15) needles
Cable needle

Tension
10 sts and 13 rows to 10 cm measured over
stocking stitch using 10mm (US 15) needles.

SPECIAL ABBREVIATIONS
C10B = slip next 5 sts onto cable needle and
leave at back of work, K5, then K5 from cable
needle; **C10F** = slip next 5 sts onto cable
needle and leave at front of work, K5, then K5
from cable needle.

SHRUG
Cast on 30 (32: 34: 36: 38: 40) sts using
10mm (US 15) needles.
Row 1 (RS): K6 (7: 6: 7: 6: 7), P2, *K2,
P2, rep from * to last 6 (7: 6: 7: 6: 7) sts,
K6 (7: 6: 7: 6: 7).
Row 2: K5, P1 (2: 1: 2: 1: 2), K2, *P2, K2,
rep from * to last 6 (7: 6: 7: 6: 7) sts,
P1 (2: 1: 2: 1: 2), K5.
These 2 rows set the sts – centre sts in rib
with 5 sts in garter st at each end of row.
Cont as set for a further 30 rows, ending
with a WS row.
Sizes XS, S and M
Next row (inc) (RS): K6 (6: 5), *K1 (1: 2),
M1, K1 (2: 3), M1, K1, rep from * 5 (4: 3)
times more, K6 (6: 5). 42 (42: 42) sts.
Next row: K5, P to last 5 sts, K5.
Sizes L, XL and XXL
Next row (inc) (RS): K6 (6: 7), M1, *(K1, M1)
4 (1: 1) times, (K2, M1) 1 (1: 2) times, rep
from * 3 (8: 4) times more, (K1, M1) 0 (0: 1)
times, K6 (5: 7). 57 (57: 57) sts.
Next row: K5, P to last 5 sts, K5.
Sizes S, M, XL and XXL
Next row: Knit.
Next row: K5, P to last 5 sts, K5.
Rep last 2 rows – (0: 1: -: 0: 1) times more.
All sizes
Now work in patt as folls:
Row 1 (RS): K6, (C10F, K5) 2 (2: 2: 3: 3: 3)
times, K6.
Row 2 and every foll alt row: K5, P to last
5 sts, K5.
Row 3: Knit.
Row 5: Knit.
Row 7: K6, (K5, C10B) 2 (2: 2: 3: 3: 3)
times, K6.
Row 9: Knit.
Row 11: Knit.
Row 12: As row 2.
These 12 rows form patt.
Cont in patt for a further 38 (40: 42: 50:
52: 54) rows, ending after patt row 2 (4: 6:
2: 4: 6) and a WS row.
Sizes XS, S and M
Next row (dec) (RS): K6 (6: 5), *K0 (0: 1),
K2tog, K0 (1: 2), K2tog, K1, rep from * 5 (4:
3) times more, K6 (6: 5). 30 (32: 34) sts.

Sizes L and XL
Next row (dec) (RS): K5, *(K2tog) 4 (2) times,
K1, rep from * 3 (8) times more, (K2tog) 5 (1)
times, K6 (5). 36 (38)sts.
Size XXL
Next row (dec) (RS): K6, (K2tog, K1, K2tog,
K2tog, K1) 5 times, (K2tog, K1) twice, K5.
40 sts.
All sizes
Next row (WS): K5, P1 (2: 1: 2: 1: 2), K2,
*P2, K2, rep from * to last 6 (7: 6: 7: 6: 7) sts,
P1 (2: 1: 2: 1: 2), K5.
Next row: K6 (7: 6: 7: 6: 7), P2, *K2, P2, rep
from * to last 6 (7: 6: 7: 6: 7) sts, K6 (7: 6: 7:
6: 7).
These 2 rows set the sts – centre sts in rib
with 5 sts in garter st at each end of row.
Cont as set for a further 29 rows, ending
with a WS row.
Cast off in patt.

MAKING UP
Press using a warm iron over a damp cloth.
Join row-end edges of first 32 rows using
back stitch, or mattress stitch if preferred,
to form first sleeve seam, reversing seam for
first 18 rows for turn-back. In same way, join
row-end edges of last 32 rows to form other
sleeve seam.

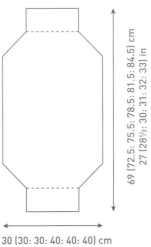

69 [72.5: 75.5: 78.5: 81.5: 84.5] cm
27 [28½: 30: 31: 32: 33] in

30 [30: 30: 40: 40: 40] cm
12 [12: 12: 16: 16: 16] in

Recommendation
Suitable for the more experienced knitter
Please see pages 38, 39 & 54 for photographs.

	XS	S	M	L	XL	XXL	
To fit	**81**	**86**	**91**	**97**	**102**	**109**	**cm**
bust	32	34	36	38	40	43	in

Rowan Kidsilk Haze
| | 6 | 7 | 7 | 7 | 8 | 8 | x 25gm |
Photographed in Fern

Needles
1 pair 2¾mm (no 12) (US 2) needles
1 pair 3¼mm (no 10) (US 3) needles

Beads – 1404 (1484: 1556: 1664: 1752: 1876) small glass beads

Tension
25 sts and 34 rows to 10 cm measured over stocking stitch using 3¼mm (US 3) needles.

EMERALD
FROTHY SWEATER WITH LACY BEADED FRILLS

BACK
Top frill (worked in 3 sections, then joined)
First section
Thread 64 (68: 72: 78: 82: 88) beads onto yarn.
Using 3¼mm (US 3) needles, work beaded cast-on as folls: cast on 1 st (onto left needle), *slide a bead up close to st on left needle, insert right needle point into st on left needle as if to K this st, take yarn round needle, draw loop through and place this loop onto left needle – 1 beaded st cast on, cast on 1 st (without a bead), rep from * until there are 129 (137: 145: 157: 165: 177) sts on left needle.
Row 1 (RS): K1, *K2, lift 2nd st on right needle over first st and off right needle, rep from * to end. 65 (69: 73: 79: 83: 89) sts.
Row 2: Knit.
Row 3: K2 (1: 3: 3: 2: 2), (K1, yfwd, K1) all into next st, (K1 wrapping yarn twice round needle) 5 times, *(K1, yfwd, K1, yfwd, K1) all into next st, (K1 wrapping yarn twice round needle) 5 times, rep from * to last 3 (2: 4: 4: 3: 3) sts, (K1, yfwd, K1) all into next st, K2 (1: 3: 3: 2: 2).
Row 4: K5 (4: 6: 6: 5: 5), slip next 5 sts from left needle to right needle dropping extra loops, slip same 5 sts back onto left needle and P these 5 sts tog, *K5, slip next 5 sts from left needle to right needle dropping extra loops, slip same 5 sts back onto left needle and P these 5 sts tog, rep from * to last 5 (4: 6: 6: 5: 5) sts, K5 (4: 6: 6: 5: 5).
Row 5: Knit.
Row 6: Purl.
Break yarn and leave sts on a holder.
Second section
Work as given for first section.
Third section
Work as given for first section until row 6 has been completed.
Join sections
Row 7 (RS): (K2tog) 0 (0: 0: 1: 1: 0) times, K to last st of third section, K tog last st of third section with first st of second section, K to last st of second section, K tog last st of second section with first st of first section, K to last 0 (0: 0: 2: 2: 0) sts, (K2tog) 0 (0: 0: 1: 1: 0) times.
193 (205: 217: 233: 245: 265) sts.

Beg with a P row, now work in st st as folls:
Work 3 rows, ending with a WS row.
Row 11 (RS): K1, (K2tog) to end.
97 (103: 109: 117: 123: 133) sts.
Work 1 row.
Row 13: K2, K2tog, K to last 4 sts, K2tog tbl, K2. 95 (101: 107: 115: 121: 131) sts.
Work 1 row, ending with a WS row.
Break yarn and leave sts on a holder.
Middle frill (worked in 2 sections, then joined)
First section
Thread 99 (105: 111: 119: 125: 135) beads onto yarn.
Using 3¼mm (US 3) needles, work beaded cast-on as folls: cast on 1 st (onto left needle), *slide a bead up close to st on left needle, insert right needle point into st on left needle as if to K this st, take yarn round needle, draw loop through and place this loop onto left needle – 1 beaded st cast on, cast on 1 st (without a bead), rep from * until there are 197 (209: 221: 237: 249: 269) sts on left needle, slide a bead up close to st on left needle, insert right needle point into st on left needle as if to K this st, take yarn round needle, draw loop through and place this loop onto left needle. 198 (210: 222: 238: 250: 270) sts
Row 1 (RS): *K2, lift 2nd st on right needle over first st and off right needle, rep from * to end. 99 (105: 111: 119: 125: 135) sts.
Row 2: Knit.
Row 3: K1 (1: 1: 2: 2: 1), (K1, yfwd, K1) all into next st, (K1 wrapping yarn twice round needle) 5 times, *(K1, yfwd, K1, yfwd, K1) all into next st, (K1 wrapping yarn twice round needle) 5 times, rep from * to last 2 (2: 2: 3: 3: 2) sts, (K1, yfwd, K1) all into next st, K1 (1: 1: 2: 2: 1).
Row 4: K4 (4: 4: 5: 5: 4), slip next 5 sts from left needle to right needle dropping extra loops, slip same 5 sts back onto left needle and P these 5 sts tog, *K5, slip next 5 sts from left needle to right needle dropping extra loops, slip same 5 sts back onto left needle and P these 5 sts tog, rep from * to last 4 (4: 4: 5: 5: 4) sts, K4 (4: 4: 5: 5: 4).
Row 5: Knit.
Row 6: Purl.
Break yarn and leave sts on a holder.

Second section

Work as given for first section until row 6 has been completed.

Join sections

Row 7 (RS): K across 99 (105: 111: 119: 125: 135) sts of second section, then K across 99 (105: 111: 119: 125: 135) sts of first section.
198 (210: 222: 238: 250: 270) sts.
Beg with a P row, now work in st st as folls:
Work 3 rows, ending with a WS row.
Row 11 (RS): (K2tog) to end.
99 (105: 111: 119: 125: 135) sts.
Work 3 rows, ending with a WS row.
Break yarn and leave sts on a holder.

Lower frill (worked in 3 sections, then joined)

First section

Thread 71 (75: 79: 85: 89: 95) beads onto yarn.
Using 3¼mm (US 3) needles, work beaded cast-on as folls: cast on 1 st (onto left needle),
*slide a bead up close to st on left needle, insert right needle point into st on left needle as if to K this st, take yarn round needle, draw loop through and place this loop onto left needle – 1 beaded st cast on, cast on 1 st (without a bead), rep from * until there are 141 (149: 157: 169: 177: 189) sts on left needle, slide a bead up close to st on left needle, insert right needle point into st on left needle as if to K this st, take yarn round needle, draw loop through and place this loop onto left needle.
142 (150: 158: 170: 178: 190) sts
Row 1 (RS): *K2, lift 2nd st on right needle over first st and off right needle, rep from * to end. 71 (75: 79: 85: 89: 95) sts.
Row 2: Knit.
Row 3: K2 (1: 0: 0: 2: 2), (K1, yfwd, K1) all into next st, (K1 wrapping yarn twice round needle) 5 times, *(K1, yfwd, K1, yfwd, K1) all into next st, (K1 wrapping yarn twice round needle) 5 times, rep from * to last 3 (2: 1: 1: 3: 3) sts, (K1, yfwd, K1) all into next st, K2 (1: 0: 0: 2: 2).
Row 4: K5 (4: 3: 3: 5: 5), slip next 5 sts from left needle to right needle dropping extra loops, slip same 5 sts back onto left needle and P these 5 sts tog, *K5, slip next 5 sts from left needle to right needle dropping extra loops, slip same 5 sts back onto left needle and P these 5 sts tog, rep from * to last 5 (4: 3: 3: 5: 5) sts, K5 (4: 3: 3: 5: 5).
Row 5: Knit.
Row 6: Purl, dec 1 st at centre of row.
70 (74: 78: 84: 88: 94) sts.
Break yarn and leave sts on a holder.

Second section

Work as given for first section.

Third section

Work as given for first section until row 6 has been completed.

Join sections

Row 7 (RS): (K2tog) 0 (0: 0: 1: 1: 0) times, K to last st of third section, K tog last st of third section with first st of second section, K to last st of second section, K tog last st of second section with first st of first section, K to last 0 (0: 0: 2: 2: 0) sts, (K2tog) 0 (0: 0: 1: 1: 0) times.
208 (220: 232: 248: 260: 280) sts.
Beg with a P row, now work in st st as folls:
Work 3 rows, ending with a WS row.
Row 11 (RS): (K2tog) to end.
104 (110: 116: 124: 130: 140) sts.
Work 3 rows, dec 1 st at centre of row of first of these rows and ending with a WS row.
103 (109: 115: 123: 129: 139) sts.
Row 15 (dec) (RS): K2, K2tog, K to last 4 sts, K2tog tbl, K2.
101 (107: 113: 121: 127: 137) sts.
Working all side seam decreases as set by last row, work 9 rows, dec 1 st at each end of 6th of these rows and ending with a WS row.
99 (105: 111: 119: 125: 135) sts.

Attach middle frill

Slip sts of middle frill onto a spare needle and, with WS of middle frill against RS of lower frill, join frills as folls: K tog first st of middle frill with first st of lower frill, *K tog next st of middle frill with next st of lower frill, rep from * to end.
99 (105: 111: 119: 125: 135) sts.
Working all side seam decreases as set, work 9 rows, dec 1 st at each end of 2nd of these rows and foll 6th row and ending with a WS row.
95 (101: 107: 115: 121: 131) sts.

Attach top frill

Slip sts of top frill onto a spare needle and, with WS of top frill against RS of work, join frills as folls: K tog first st of top frill with first st of joined middle and lower frills, *K tog next st of top frill with next st of joined middle and lower frills, rep from * to end.
95 (101: 107: 115: 121: 131) sts.
Place markers at both ends of last row.
Beg with a P row and working all side seam decreases as set, cont in st st as folls:
Dec 1 st at each end of 6th and 2 foll 8th rows.
89 (95: 101: 109: 115: 125) sts.
Work 21 rows, ending with a WS row.

Next row (inc) (RS): K3, M1, K to last 3 sts, M1, K3.
Working all size seam increases as set by last row, inc 1 st at each end of 10th and 4 foll 10th rows.
101 (107: 113: 121: 127: 137) sts.
Cont straight until back measures 32 (32: 33: 33: 33: 33) cm **from markers**, ending with a WS row.

Shape armholes

Cast off 5 (6: 6: 7: 7: 8) sts at beg of next 2 rows.
91 (95: 101: 107: 113: 121) sts.
Dec 1 st at each end of next 3 (3: 5: 5: 7: 9) rows, then on foll 2 (3: 3: 4: 4: 4) alt rows, then on foll 4th row.
79 (81: 83: 87: 89: 93) sts.
Cont straight until armhole measures 18 (19: 19: 20: 21: 22) cm, ending with a WS row.

Shape shoulders and back neck

Cast off 4 (4: 4: 5: 5: 6) sts at beg of next 2 rows.
71 (73: 75: 77: 79: 81) sts.
Next row (RS): Cast off 4 (4: 4: 5: 5: 6) sts, K until there are 8 (8: 9: 8: 9: 9) sts on right needle and turn, leaving rem sts on a holder.
Work each side of neck separately.
Cast off 4 sts at beg of next row.
Cast off rem 4 (4: 5: 4: 5: 5) sts.
With RS facing, rejoin yarn to rem sts, cast off centre 47 (49: 49: 51: 51: 51) sts, K to end.
Complete to match first side, reversing shapings.

FRONT

Work as given for back until 14 (14: 14: 16: 16: 16) rows less have been worked than on back to beg of shoulder shaping, ending with a WS row.

Shape front neck

Next row (RS): K21 (21: 22: 24: 25: 27) and turn, leaving rem sts on a holder.
Work each side of neck separately.
Dec 1 st at neck edge of next 6 rows, then on foll 2 (2: 2: 3: 3: 3) alt rows.
13 (13: 14: 15: 16: 18) sts.
Work 3 rows, ending with a WS row.

Shape shoulder

Cast off 4 (4: 4: 5: 5: 6) sts at beg of next and foll alt row **and at same time** dec 1 st at neck edge of next row.
Work 1 row.
Cast off rem 4 (4: 5: 4: 5: 5) sts.
With RS facing, rejoin yarn to rem sts, cast off centre 37 (39: 39: 39: 39: 39) sts, K to end.
Complete to match first side, reversing shapings.

SLEEVES (both alike)

Thread 99 (103: 103: 105: 113: 119) beads onto yarn.

Using 3¼mm (US 3) needles, work beaded cast-on as folls: cast on 1 st (onto left needle), *slide a bead up close to st on left needle, insert right needle point into st on left needle as if to K this st, take yarn round needle, draw loop through and place this loop onto left needle – 1 beaded st cast on, cast on 1 st (without a bead), rep from * until there are 197 (205: 205: 209: 225: 237) sts on left needle, slide a bead up close to st on left needle, insert right needle point into st on left needle as if to K this st, take yarn round needle, draw loop through and place this loop onto left needle.

198 (206: 206: 210: 226: 238) sts.

Row 1 (RS): *K2, lift 2nd st on right needle over first st and off right needle, rep from * to end.

99 (103: 103: 105: 113: 119) sts.

Row 2: Knit.

Row 3: K1 (0: 0: 1: 2: 2), (K1, yfwd, K1) all into next st, (K1 wrapping yarn twice round needle) 5 times, *(K1, yfwd, K1, yfwd, K1) all into next st, (K1 wrapping yarn twice round needle) 5 times, rep from * to last 2 (1: 1: 2: 3: 3) sts, (K1, yfwd, K1) all into next st, K1 (0: 0: 1: 2: 2).

Row 4: K4 (3: 3: 4: 5: 5), slip next 5 sts from left needle to right needle dropping extra loops, slip same 5 sts back onto left needle and P these 5 sts tog, *K5, slip next 5 sts from left needle to right needle dropping extra loops, slip same 5 sts back onto left needle and P these 5 sts tog, rep from * to last 4 (3: 3: 4: 5: 5) sts, K4 (3: 3: 4: 5: 5).

Beg with a K row, work in st st for 6 rows, dec (dec: dec: inc: inc: dec) 1 st at centre of first of these rows and ending with a WS row.

98 (102: 102: 106: 114: 118) sts.

Row 11 (RS): (K2tog) to end.

49 (51: 51: 53: 57: 59) sts.

Beg with a P row and working all sleeve increases in same way as side seam increases, now work in st st, shaping sides by inc 1 st at each end of 10th and every foll 10th row to 63 (75: 71: 81: 71: 81) sts, then on every foll 12th (12th: 12th: -: 12th: 12th) row until there are 73 (77: 77: -: 83: 87) sts.

Cont straight until sleeve measures 47 (48: 49: 50: 51: 52) cm from cast-on edge, ending with a WS row.

Shape top

Cast off 5 (6: 6: 7: 7: 8) sts at beg of next 2 rows.

63 (65: 65: 67: 69: 71) sts.

Dec 1 st at each end of next 3 rows, then on foll alt row, then on foll 4th row, then on 3 foll 6th rows, then on 2 foll 4th rows.

43 (45: 45: 47: 49: 51) sts.

Work 1 row.

Dec 1 st at each end of next and every foll alt row to 39 sts, then on foll 5 rows, ending with a WS row.

Cast off rem 29 sts.

MAKING UP

Pin the pieces out and steam gently without allowing the iron to touch the yarn.

Join right shoulder seam using back stitch or mattress stitch if preferred.

Neckband

With RS facing and using 2¾mm (US 2) needles, pick up and knit 18 (18: 18: 20: 20: 20) sts down left side of neck, 37 (39: 39: 39: 39: 39) sts from front, 18 (18: 18: 20: 20: 20) sts up right side of neck, then 55 (57: 57: 59: 59: 59) sts from back.

128 (132: 132: 138: 138: 138) sts.

Beg with a K row, work in rev st st for 4 rows, ending with a **RS** row.

Cast off knitwise (on **WS**).

Join left shoulder and neckband seam.

Join side seams.

Join side seams of frills, and seams within frills where sections meet.

Join sleeve seams. Insert sleeves into armholes.

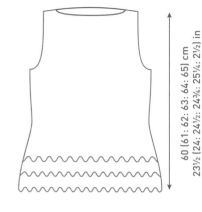

60 (61: 62: 63: 64: 65) cm
23½ (24: 24½: 24¾: 25¼: 25½) in

47 (48: 49: 50: 51: 52) cm
18½ (19: 19¼: 19¾: 20: 20½) in

RAVEN
CHIC TAILORED JACKET

Recommendation
Suitable for the knitter with a little experience
Please see pages 26 & 27 for photographs.

	XS	S	M	L	XL	XXL	
To fit	**81**	**86**	**91**	**97**	**102**	**109**	cm
bust	32	34	36	38	40	43	in

Rowan Wool Cotton
| | 11 | 12 | 12 | 13 | 13 | 14 | x 50gm |

Photographed in Inky

Needles
1 pair 3¼mm (no 10) (US 3) needles
1 pair 3¾mm (no 9) (US 5) needles

Buttons · 9

Tension
23 sts and 38 rows to 10 cm measured over
moss stitch using 3¾mm (US 5) needles.

BACK
Cast on 91 (97: 103: 109: 115: 125) sts
using 3¼mm (US 3) needles.
Work in garter st for 3 rows, end with a **RS** row.
Change to 3¾mm (US 5) needles.
Row 4 (WS): K1, *P1, K1, rep from * to end.
Row 5: As row 4.
Last 2 rows form moss st.
Work in moss st for a further 29 (29: 31:
31: 31: 31) rows, dec 1 st at each end of
16th (16th: 18th: 18th: 18th: 18th) of these
rows and ending with a WS row.
89 (95: 101: 107: 113: 123) sts.
Shape darts
Counting in from both ends of last row,
place markers on 21st (23rd: 25th: 27th:
29th: 31st) sts in from both ends of row.
Next row (dec) (RS): Work 2 tog, moss st
to within 1 st of marked st, work 3 tog tbl
(marked st is centre st of these 3 sts), moss
st to within 1 st of next marked st, work 3 tog
(marked st is centre st of these 3 sts), moss
st to last 2 sts, work 2 tog.
83 (89: 95: 101: 107: 117) sts.
Work 13 rows.
Rep last 14 rows once more, then first of
these rows (the dec row) again.
71 (77: 83: 89: 95: 105) sts.
Work 21 rows, ending with RS facing for next row.
Next row (inc) (RS): Inc in first st, *moss st to
marked st, M1, patt marked st, M1, rep from
* once more, moss st to last st, inc in last st.
77 (83: 89: 95: 101: 111) sts.
Work 13 rows.
Rep last 14 rows once more, then first
of these rows (the inc row) again.
89 (95: 101: 107: 113: 123) sts.
Inc 1 st at each end of 14th and foll
12th (12th: 14th: 14th: 14th: 14th) row.
93 (99: 105: 111: 117: 127) sts.
Work 9 rows, ending with a WS row. (Back
should measure 39 (39: 40: 40: 40: 40) cm.)
Shape armholes
Cast off 3 (4: 4: 5: 5: 6) sts at beg of next
2 rows. 87 (91: 97: 101: 107: 115) sts.
Dec 1 st at each end of next 5 (5: 7: 7: 9: 11)
rows, then on foll 2 (3: 3: 4: 4: 4) alt rows, then
on foll 4th row. 71 (73: 75: 77: 79: 83) sts.
Cont straight until armhole measures 17 (18:
18: 18: 19: 20: 21) cm, ending with a WS row.

Shape shoulders and back neck
Cast off 6 (7: 7: 7: 7: 8) sts at beg of next
2 rows. 59 (59: 61: 63: 65: 67) sts.
Next row (RS): Cast off 6 (7: 7: 7: 7: 8) sts,
moss st until there are 11 (10: 11: 10: 11:
11) sts on right needle and turn, leaving
rem sts on a holder.
Work each side of neck separately.
Cast off 4 sts at beg of next row.
Cast off rem 7 (6: 7: 6: 7: 7) sts.
With RS facing, rejoin yarn to rem sts, cast
off centre 25 (25: 25: 29: 29: 29) sts, moss
st to end.
Complete to match first side, rev shapings.

LEFT FRONT
Cast on 52 (55: 58: 61: 64: 69) sts using
3¼mm (US 3) needles.
Work in garter st for 3 rows, ending with
a **RS** row.
Change to 3¾mm (US 5) needles.
Row 4 (WS): *K1, P1, rep from * to last
0 (1: 0: 1: 0: 1) st, K0 (1: 0: 1: 0: 1).
Row 5: K0 (1: 0: 1: 0: 1), *P1, K1, rep from *
to end.
Last 2 rows form moss st.
Work in moss st for a further 29 (29: 31: 31:
31: 31) rows, dec 1 st at beg of 16th (16th:
18th: 18th: 18th: 18th) of these rows and end
with a WS row. 51 (54: 57: 60: 63: 68) sts.
Shape dart
Counting in from end of last row, place
marker on 21st (23rd: 25th: 27th: 29th: 31st)
st in from end of row.
Next row (dec) (RS): Work 2 tog, moss st
to within 1 st of marked st, work 3 tog tbl
(marked st is centre st of these 3 sts), moss
st to end. 48 (51: 54: 57: 60: 65) sts.
Work 13 rows.
Rep last 14 rows once more, then first of
these rows (the dec row) again.
42 (45: 48: 51: 54: 59) sts.
Work 21 rows, ending with RS facing for
next row.
Next row (inc) (RS): Inc in first st, moss st to
marked st, M1, patt marked st, M1, moss st
to end. 45 (48: 51: 54: 57: 62) sts.
Work 13 rows, then rep the dart inc row once
more. 48 (51: 54: 57: 60: 65) sts.
Work 1 row, ending with a WS row.

Shape front slope.

Next row (RS): Moss st to last 13 sts, work 3 tog tbl (for front slope dec), moss st 10 sts. 46 (49: 52: 55: 58: 63) sts.

Working all front slope decreases as set by last row, cont as folls:

Work 11 rows, ending with a WS row.

Rep the dart inc row once more. 49 (52: 55: 58: 61: 66) sts.

Dec 2 sts at front slope edge of 4th (4th: 4th: 2nd: 2nd: 4th) and 1 (1: 2: 2: 2: 2) foll 16th (16th: 16th: 14th: 16th: 16th) rows **and at same time** inc 1 st at side seam edge of 14th and foll · (·: 14th: 14th: 14th: 14th) row. 46 (49: 51: 54: 57: 62) sts.

Work 15 (15: 1: 7: 3: 1) rows, inc 1 (1: 0: 0: 0: 0) st at beg of 6th of these rows and ending with a WS row.

47 (50: 51: 54: 57: 62) sts.

Shape armhole

Cast off 3 (4: 4: 5: 5: 6) sts at beg and dec 2 (2: 0: 0: 0: 0) sts at front slope edge of next row. 42 (44: 47: 49: 52: 56) sts.

Work 1 row.

Dec 1 st at armhole edge of next 5 (5: 7: 7: 9: 11) rows, then on foll 2 (3: 3: 4: 4: 4) alt rows, then on foll 4th row **and at same time** dec 2 sts at front slope edge of 0 (15th: 13th: 7th: 11th: 13th) row. 34 (33: 34: 35: 36: 38) sts.

Dec 2 sts at front slope edge **only** on 2nd (16th: 14th: 4th: 6th: 6th) and 2 (1: 1: 2: 2: 2) foll 16th (18th: 18th: 16th: 16th: 16th) rows. 28 (29: 30: 29: 30: 32) sts.

Cont straight until left front matches back to beg of shoulder shaping, ending with a WS row.

Shape shoulder

Cast off 6 (7: 7: 7: 7: 8) sts at beg of next and foll alt row, then 7 (6: 7: 6: 7: 7) sts at beg of foll alt row. 9 sts.

Inc 1 st at end of next row. 10 sts.

Cont in moss st on these 10 sts only (for back neck border extension) for a further 7 (7: 7: 8: 8: 8) cm, ending with a WS row.

Cast off in moss st.

RIGHT FRONT

Cast on 52 (55: 58: 61: 64: 69) sts using 3¼mm (US 3) needles.

Work in garter st for 3 rows, ending with a **RS** row.

Change to 3¾mm (US 5) needles.

Row 4 (WS): K0 (1: 0: 1: 0: 1), *P1, K1, rep from * to end.

Row 5: *K1, P1, rep from * to last 0 (1: 0: 1: 0: 1) st, K0 (1: 0: 1: 0: 1).

Last 2 rows form moss st.

Work in moss st for a further 15 (15: 17: 17: 17: 17) rows, ending with a WS row.

Next row (buttonhole row) (RS): Moss st 4 sts, cast off 2 sts (to make a buttonhole – cast on 2 sts over these cast-off sts on next row), moss st to last 2 sts, work 2 tog. 51 (54: 57: 60: 63: 68) sts.

Making a further 4 buttonholes in this way on every foll 18th row from previous buttonhole and noting that no further reference will be made to buttonholes, cont as folls:

Work 13 rows, ending with a WS row.

Shape dart

Counting in from beg of last row, place marker on 21st (23rd: 25th: 27th: 29th: 31st) st in from beg of row.

Next row (dec) (RS): Moss st to within 1 st of marked st, work 3 tog (marked st is centre st of these 3 sts), moss st to last 2 sts, work 2 tog.

48 (51: 54: 57: 60: 65) sts.

Work 13 rows.

Rep last 14 rows once more, then first of these rows (the dec row) again.

42 (45: 48: 51: 54: 59) sts.

Work 21 rows, ending with RS facing for next row.

Next row (inc) (RS): Moss st to marked st, M1, patt marked st, M1, moss st to last st, inc in last st.

45 (48: 51: 54: 57: 62) sts.

Work 13 rows, then rep the dart inc row once more. 48 (51: 54: 57: 60: 65) sts.

Work 1 row, ending with a WS row.

Shape front slope.

Next row (RS): Moss st 10 sts, work 3 tog (for front slope dec), moss st to end. 46 (49: 52: 55: 58: 63) sts.

Working all front slope decreases as set by last row, complete to match left front, reversing shapings.

LEFT SLEEVE

Front sleeve

Cast on 25 (26: 27: 28: 29: 30) sts using 3¼mm (US 3) needles.

Work in garter st for 3 rows, ending with a **RS** row.

Change to 3¾mm (US 9) needles.

Row 4 (WS): *K1, P1, rep from * to last 1 (0: 1: 0: 1: 0) st, K1 (0: 1: 0: 1: 0).

Row 5: K1 (0: 1: 0: 1: 0), *P1, K1, rep from * to end.

These 2 rows form moss st.

Cont in moss st, inc 1 st at end of 10th and foll 10th (10th: 12th: 10th: 10th: 10th) row. 27 (28: 29: 30: 31: 32) sts.

Work 7 (7: 5: 7: 7: 7) rows, ending with a WS row.

Break yarn and leave sts on a holder.

Back sleeve

Cast on 25 (26: 27: 28: 29: 30) sts using 3¼mm (US 3) needles.

Work in garter st for 3 rows, ending with a **RS** row.

Change to 3¾mm (US 9) needles.

Row 4 (WS): K1 (0: 1: 0: 1: 0), *P1, K1, rep from * to end.

Row 5: *K1, P1, rep from * to last 1 (0: 1: 0: 1: 0) st, K1 (0: 1: 0: 1: 0).

These 2 rows form moss st.

Cont in moss st, inc 1 st at beg of 10th and foll 10th (10th: 12th: 10th: 10th: 10th) row. 27 (28: 29: 30: 31: 32) sts.

Work 7 (7: 5: 7: 7: 7) rows, ending with a WS row.

Join sections

Next row (RS): Moss st to last 7 sts of sleeve back, holding WS of sleeve front against RS of sleeve back, work tog first st of sleeve front with next st of sleeve back, (work tog next st of sleeve front with next st of sleeve back) 6 times, moss st to end. 47 (49: 51: 53: 55: 57) sts.

**Cont in moss st, inc 1 st at each end of 2nd (2nd: 6th: 2nd: 4th: 2nd) and every foll 12th (10th: 12th: 12th: 12th: 10th) row to 69 (61: 71: 77: 79: 65) sts, then on every foll · (12th: 14th: ·: ·: 12th) row until there are · (73: 73: ·: ·: 83) sts.

Cont straight until sleeve measures 45 (46: 47: 48: 49: 50) cm, ending with a WS row.

40.5 (43: 45.5: 48.5: 51: 55) cm
16 (17: 18: 19: 20: 21½) in

56 (57: 58: 59: 60: 61) cm
22 (22½: 22¾: 23¼: 23½: 24) in

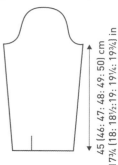

45 (46: 47: 48: 49: 50) cm
17¾ (18: 18½: 19: 19¼: 19¾) in

Continued on next page...

Recommendation
Suitable for the knitter with a little experience
Please see page 20 for photograph.

Rowan Kidsilk Haze
A 1 x 25gm
B 1 x 25gm
Photographed in Blood & Liqueur

Needles
1 pair 3¼mm (no 10) (US 3) needles

Beads – 442 small glass beads

Tension
23 sts and 35 rows to 10 cm measured over
pattern using 3¼mm (US 3) needles.

Finished size
Completed scarf measures approx 220 cm
(86½ in) long and 9 cm (3½ in) wide.

EVE
STRIPY SCARF WITH LACY FLOUNCE EDGING

SCARF
First section
Thread 221 beads onto yarn A.
Using 3¼mm (US 3) needles and yarn A,
work beaded cast-on as folls: cast on 1 st (onto
left needle), *slide a bead up close to st on left
needle, insert right needle point into st on left
needle as if to K this st, take yarn round needle,
draw loop through and place this loop onto left
needle – 1 beaded st cast on, rep from * until
there are 222 sts on left needle.
Row 1 (RS): *K2, lift 2nd st on right
needle over first st and off right needle,
rep from * to end. 111 sts.
Row 2: Knit.
Join in yarn B.
Row 3: Using yarn B, K1, (K1, yfwd, K1) all
into next st, (K1 wrapping yarn twice round
needle) 5 times, *(K1, yfwd, K1, yfwd, K1)
all into next st, (K1 wrapping yarn twice round
needle) 5 times, rep from * to last 2 sts, (K1,
yfwd, K1) all into next st, K1.
Row 4: Using yarn B, K4, slip next 5 sts from
left needle to right needle dropping extra loops,
slip same 5 sts back onto left needle and P
these 5 sts tog, *K5, slip next 5 sts from left
needle to right needle dropping extra loops,
slip same 5 sts back onto left needle and P
these 5 sts tog, rep from * to last 4 sts, K4.
Break off yarn B.
Using yarn A and beg with a K row, now work
in st st as folls:
Work 6 rows, ending with a WS row.

Row 11 (RS): K1, (K2tog) to end. 56 sts.
Work 6 rows, ending with a RS row.
Row 18 (WS): (P2tog) to end. 28 sts.
These 18 rows complete flounce.
Join in yarn B and now work in patt as folls:
Row 1 (RS): Using yarn B, inc in first st,
K to last 2 sts, K2tog.
Row 2: Using yarn B, knit.
Rows 3 and 4: As rows 1 and 2.
Row 5: Using yarn A, inc in first st, (K1, yfwd,
K1) all into next st, (K1 wrapping yarn twice
round needle) 5 times, *(K1, yfwd, K1, yfwd,
K1) all into next st, (K1 wrapping yarn twice
round needle) 5 times, rep from * 3 times
more, (K1, yfwd, K1) all into next st, K2tog.
Row 6: Using yarn A, K4, slip next 5 sts from
left needle to right needle dropping extra loops,
slip same 5 sts back onto left needle and P
these 5 sts tog, *K5, slip next 5 sts from left
needle to right needle dropping extra loops,
slip same 5 sts back onto left needle and P
these 5 sts tog, rep from * to last 5 sts, K5.
These 6 rows form patt.
Cont in patt until work measures approx
110 cm, ending after patt row 2.**
Break yarn and leave sts on a holder.
Second section
Work as given for first section to **.
Join sections
Holding sections with RS facing, cast off both
sets of sts together by taking one st from one
section together with corresponding st from
other section.

Raven - Continued from previous page ...

Shape top
Cast off 3 (4: 4: 5: 5: 6) sts at beg of
next 2 rows.
63 (65: 65: 67: 69: 71) sts.
Dec 1 st at each end of next 3 rows, then
on foll alt row, then on foll 4th row, then
on 4 foll 6th rows.
45 (47: 47: 49: 51: 53) sts.
Work 3 rows.
Dec 1 st at each end of next and every foll alt
row to 37 sts, then on foll 5 rows, ending with
a WS row.
Cast off rem 27 sts.

RIGHT SLEEVE
Back sleeve
Work as given for front sleeve of left sleeve.
Front sleeve
Work as given for back sleeve of left sleeve.
Join sections
Next row (RS): Moss st to last 7 sts of sleeve
front, holding WS of sleeve front against RS
of sleeve back, work tog next st of sleeve front
with first st of sleeve back, (work tog next st of
sleeve front with next st of sleeve back) 6 times,
moss st to end. 47 (49: 51: 53: 55: 57) sts.
Complete as given for left sleeve from **.

MAKING UP
Pin the pieces out and steam gently without
allowing the iron to touch the yarn.
Join both shoulder seams using back stitch
or mattress stitch if preferred. Join cast-off
edges of back neck border extensions, then
sew one edge to back neck.
Join side seams.
Join sleeve seams. Insert sleeves into
armholes.
Sew on buttons, attaching 2 buttons to each
cuff through edges of both sleeve front and
back as in photograph.

Recommendation

Suitable for the knitter with a little experience
Please see pages 50, 52 & 54 for photographs.

	XS	S	M	L	XL	XXL	
To fit	**81**	**86**	**91**	**97**	**102**	**109**	cm
bust	32	34	36	38	40	43	in

Rowan Kidsilk Haze

| A | 4 | 4 | 5 | 5 | 6 | 6 | x 25gm |
| B | 1 | 1 | 1 | 1 | 1 | 1 | x 25gm |

Photographed in Splendour with Blackcurrant

Needles

1 pair 2¾mm (no 12) (US 2) needles
1 pair 3mm (no 11) (US 2/3) needles
1 pair 3¼mm (no 10) (US 3) needles

Buttons – 7

Tension

25 sts and 34 rows to 10 cm measured over
stocking stitch using 3¼mm (US 3) needles.

GARNET

NEAT CARDIGAN WITH FRONT RUFFLE TRIMS

BACK

Cast on 166 (178: 190: 206: 218: 238) sts
using 2¾mm (US 2) needles and yarn A.
Row 1 (RS): (K2tog) 0 (1: 0: 2: 0: 0) times,
(P2tog) 1 (3: 1: 3: 2: 1) times, *(K2tog) 3
times, (P2tog) 3 times, rep from * to last
8 (2: 8: 4: 10: 8) sts, (K2tog) 3 (1: 3: 2:
3: 3) times, (P2tog) 1 (0: 1: 0: 2: 1) times.
83 (89: 95: 103: 109: 119) sts.
Row 2: P0 (1: 0: 2: 0: 0), K1 (3: 1: 3: 2: 1),
*P3, K3, rep from * to last 4 (1: 4: 2: 5: 4)
sts, P3 (1: 3: 2: 3: 3), K1 (0: 1: 0: 2: 1).
Row 3: K0 (1: 0: 2: 0: 0), P1 (3: 1: 3: 2: 1),
*K3, P3, rep from * to last 4 (1: 4: 2: 5: 4)
sts, K3 (1: 3: 2: 3: 3), P1 (0: 1: 0: 2: 1).
Rows 2 and 3 form rib.
Work in rib for a further 13 rows, inc 1 st
at each end of 10th of these rows and
ending with a WS row.
85 (91: 97: 105: 111: 121) sts.
Change to 3¼mm (US 3) needles.
Beg with a K row, cont in st st as folls:
Work 4 rows, ending with a WS row.
Next row (inc) (RS): K3, M1, K to last
3 sts, M1, K3.
Working all size seam increases as set by last
row, inc 1 st at each end of 8th and 6 foll 6th
rows. 101 (107: 113: 121: 127: 137) sts.
Work 7 (7: 11: 11: 11: 11) rows, ending with
a WS row. (Back should measure 21 (21: 22:
22: 22: 22) cm.)
Shape armholes
Cast off 5 (6: 6: 7: 7: 8) sts at beg of next
2 rows.
91 (95: 101: 107: 113: 121) sts.
Dec 1 st at each end of next 5 (5: 7: 7:
9: 11) rows, then on foll 1 (2: 2: 3: 3: 3)
alt rows, then on foll 4th row.
77 (79: 81: 85: 87: 91) sts.
Work 45 (47: 45: 45: 47: 49) rows, ending
with a WS row. (Armhole should measure
17 (18: 18: 19: 20: 21) cm.)
Shape shoulders and back neck
Cast off 7 (7: 7: 8: 8: 8) sts at beg of next
2 rows.
63 (65: 67: 69: 71: 75) sts.
Next row (RS): Cast off 7 (7: 7: 8: 8: 8) sts,
K until there are 11 (11: 12: 11: 12: 13) sts
on right needle and turn, leaving rem sts
on a holder.

Work each side of neck separately.
Cast off 4 sts at beg of next row.
Cast off rem 7 (7: 8: 7: 8: 9) sts.
With RS facing, rejoin yarn to rem sts,
cast off centre 27 (29: 29: 31: 31: 33) sts,
K to end.
Complete to match first side, reversing
shapings.

LEFT FRONT

Cast on 92 (98: 104: 112: 118: 128) sts
using 2¾mm (US 2) needles and yarn A.
Row 1 (RS): (K2tog) 0 (1: 0: 2: 0: 0) times,
(P2tog) 1 (3: 1: 3: 2: 1) times, *(K2tog) 3
times, (P2tog) 3 times, rep from * to last
18 sts, (K2tog) twice, (P2tog) 7 times.
46 (49: 52: 56: 59: 64) sts.
Row 2: K7, P2, K3, *P3, K3, rep from * to
last 4 (1: 4: 2: 5: 4) sts, P3 (1: 3: 2: 3: 3),
K1 (0: 1: 0: 2: 1).
Row 3: K0 (1: 0: 2: 0: 0), P1 (3: 1: 3: 2: 1),
*K3, P3, rep from * to last 9 sts, K2, P7.
Row 4: P9, K3, *P3, K3, rep from * to last
4 (1: 4: 2: 5: 4) sts, P3 (1: 3: 2: 3: 3),
K1 (0: 1: 0: 2: 1).
Row 5: K0 (1: 0: 2: 0: 0), P1 (3: 1: 3: 2: 1),
*K3, P3, rep from * to last 9 sts, K9.
Row 6: P9, K3, *P3, K3, rep from * to last
4 (1: 4: 2: 5: 4) sts, P3 (1: 3: 2: 3: 3),
K1 (0: 1: 0: 2: 1).
Row 7: K0 (1: 0: 2: 0: 0), P1 (3: 1: 3: 2: 1),
*K3, P3, rep from * to last 9 sts, K2, P7.
Rows 2 to 7 set the sts – front opening edge
7 sts in ridge patt with all other sts in rib.
Cont as set for a further 9 rows, inc 1 st
at beg of 6th of these rows and ending
with a WS row.
47 (50: 53: 57: 60: 65) sts.
Change to 3¼mm (US 3) needles.
Row 17 (RS): K to last 7 sts, patt 7 sts.
Row 18: Patt 7 sts, P to end.
Last 2 rows set the sts – front opening edge
7 sts still in ridge patt with all other sts now
in st st.
Working all size seam increases as set by
back and keeping sts correct as now set,
cont as folls:
Inc 1 st at beg of 3rd and foll 8th row.
49 (52: 55: 59: 62: 67) sts.
Work 1 row, ending with a WS row.

Place first frill placement line

Next row (RS): K to last 12 sts, P1 (for frill placement line), K4, patt 7 sts.

Next row: Patt 7 sts, P4, K1, P to end.

These 2 rows set position of first frill placement line.

Keeping sts correct as now set, work 8 rows, inc 1 st at beg of 3rd of these rows.

50 (53: 56: 60: 63: 68) sts.

Place second frill placement line

Next row (RS): K3, M1, K to last 20 sts, P1 (for 2nd frill placement line), patt to end.

51 (54: 57: 61: 64: 69) sts.

Next row: Patt 19 sts, K1, P to end.

These 2 rows set position of second frill placement line.

Keeping sts correct as now set, work 8 rows, inc 1 st at beg of 5th of these rows.

52 (55: 58: 62: 65: 70) sts.

Place third frill placement line

Next row (RS): K to last 28 sts, P1 (for 3rd frill placement line), patt to end.

Next row: Patt 27 sts, K1, P to end.

These 2 rows set position of third frill placement line.

Keeping sts correct as now set throughout, cont as folls:

Inc 1 st at beg of next and 2 foll 6th rows.

55 (58: 61: 65: 68: 73) sts.

Work 7 (7: 11: 11: 11: 11) rows, ending with a WS row.

Shape armhole

Keeping sts correct, cast off 5 (6: 6: 7: 7: 8) sts at beg of next 2 rows.

50 (52: 55: 58: 61: 65) sts.

Work 1 row.

Dec 1 st at armhole edge of next 5 (5: 7: 7: 9: 11) rows, then on foll 1 (2: 2: 3: 3: 3) alt rows, then on foll 4th row.

43 (44: 45: 47: 48: 50) sts.

Work 29 (27: 21: 19: 23: 21) rows, ending with a WS row.

Shape neck

Next row (RS): Patt 30 (31: 32: 34: 35: 36) sts and turn, leaving rem 13 (13: 13: 13: 13: 14) sts on a holder.

Keeping sts correct, dec 1 st at neck edge of next 6 rows, then on foll 2 (2: 2: 3: 3: 3) alt rows, then on 1 (2: 2: 2: 2: 2) foll 4th rows. 21 (21: 22: 23: 24: 25) sts.

Work 1 (1: 5: 5: 3: 7) rows, ending with a WS row.

Shape shoulder

Cast off 7 (7: 7: 8: 8: 8) sts at beg of next and foll alt row.

Work 1 row.

Cast off rem 7 (7: 8: 7: 8: 9) sts.

RIGHT FRONT

Cast on 92 (98: 104: 112: 118: 128) sts using 2¾mm (US 2) needles and yarn A.

Row 1 (RS): (P2tog) 7 times, (K2tog) twice, *(P2tog) 3 times, (K2tog) 3 times, rep from * to last 2 (8: 2: 10: 4: 2) sts, (P2tog) 1 (3: 1: 3: 2: 1) times, (K2tog) 0 (1: 0: 2: 0: 0) times.

46 (49: 52: 56: 59: 64) sts.

Row 2: K1 (0: 1: 0: 2: 1), P3 (1: 3: 2: 3: 3), *K3, P3, rep from * to last 12 sts, K3, P2, K7.

Row 3: P7, K2, *P3, K3, rep from * to last 1 (4: 1: 5: 2: 1) sts, P1 (3: 1: 3: 2: 1), K0 (1: 0: 2: 0: 0).

Row 4: K1 (0: 1: 0: 2: 1), P3 (1: 3: 2: 3: 3), *K3, P3, rep from * to last 12 sts, K3, P9.

Row 5 (buttonhole row): K2, K2tog, yfwd (to make a buttonhole), K5, *P3, K3, rep from * to last 1 (4: 1: 5: 2: 1) sts, P1 (3: 1: 3: 2: 1), K0 (1: 0: 2: 0: 0).

Working a further 6 buttonholes in this way on 12th (12th: 12th: 12th: 18th: 18th) and every foll 18th row and noting that no further reference will be made to buttonholes, cont as folls:

Row 6: K1 (0: 1: 0: 2: 1), P3 (1: 3: 2: 3: 3), *K3, P3, rep from * to last 12 sts, K3, P9.

Row 7: P7, K2, *P3, K3, rep from * to last 1 (4: 1: 5: 2: 1) sts, P1 (3: 1: 3: 2: 1), K0 (1: 0: 2: 0: 0).

Rows 2 to 7 set the sts – front opening edge 7 sts in ridge patt with all other sts in rib.

Cont as set for a further 9 rows, inc 1 st at end of 6th of these rows and ending with a WS row.

47 (50: 53: 57: 60: 65) sts.

Change to 3¼mm (US 3) needles.

Row 17 (RS): Patt 7 sts, K to end.

Row 18: P to last 7 sts, patt 7 sts.

Last 2 rows set the sts – front opening edge 7 sts still in ridge patt with all other sts now in st st.

Working all size seam increases as set by back and keeping sts correct as now set, cont as folls:

Inc 1 st at end of 3rd and foll 8th row.

49 (52: 55: 59: 62: 67) sts.

Work 1 row, ending with a WS row.

Place first frill placement line

Next row (RS): Patt 7 sts, K4, P1 (for frill placement line), K to end.

Next row: P to last 12 sts, K1, P4, patt 7 sts.

These 2 rows set position of first frill placement line.

Keeping sts correct as now set, work 8 rows, inc 1 st at end of 3rd of these rows.

50 (53: 56: 60: 63: 68) sts.

Place second frill placement line

Next row (RS): Patt 19 sts, P1 (for 2nd frill placement line), K to last 3 sts, M1, K3.

51 (54: 57: 61: 64: 69) sts.

Next row: P to last 20 sts, K1, patt 19 sts.

These 2 rows set position of second frill placement line.

Keeping sts correct as now set, work 8 rows, inc 1 st at end of 5th of these rows.

52 (55: 58: 62: 65: 70) sts.

Place third frill placement line

Next row (RS): Patt 27 sts, P1 (for 3rd frill placement line), K to end.

Next row: P to last 28 sts, K1, patt to end.

These 2 rows set position of third frill placement line.

Keeping sts correct as now set throughout, complete to match left front, reversing shapings and working first row of neck shaping as folls:

Shape neck

Next row (RS): Patt 13 (13: 13: 13: 13: 14) sts and slip these sts onto a holder, patt to end. 30 (31: 32: 34: 35: 36) sts.

SLEEVES (both alike)

Cast on 188 (196: 196: 204: 220: 228) sts using 3mm (US 2/3) needles and yarn B **DOUBLE**.

Break off yarn B and join in yarn A.

(**Note:** Yarn is used single from this point on.)

Row 1 (RS): *sl 1, K1, psso, rep from * to end. 94 (98: 98: 102: 110: 114) sts.

Row 2: Purl.

Row 3: As row 1. 47 (49: 49: 51: 55: 57) sts.

Beg with a P row, now work in st st throughout as folls:

Work 3 rows, ending with a WS row.

Place markers at both ends of last row.

Change to 3¼mm (US 3) needles.

Working all sleeve increases in same way as side seam increases, cont in st st, shaping sides by inc 1 st at each end of 9th (9th: 9th: 7th: 9th: 9th) and every foll 10th (10th: 10th: 8th: 10th: 10th) row to 67 (77: 77: 59: 77: 87) sts, then on every foll 12th (-: -: 10th: 12th: -) row until there are 73 (-: -: 81: 83: -) sts.

Cont straight until sleeve measures 45 (46: 47: 48: 49: 50) cm **from markers**, ending with a WS row.

Shape top

Cast off 5 (6: 6: 7: 7: 8) sts at beg of next 2 rows. 63 (65: 65: 67: 69: 71) sts.

Dec 1 st at each end of next 3 rows, then on foll alt row, then on 7 foll 4th rows. 41 (43: 43: 45: 47: 49) sts.

Work 1 row.

Dec 1 st at each end of next and every foll alt
row to 37 sts, then on foll 3 rows, ending with
a WS row.
Cast off rem 31 sts.

MAKING UP
Pin the pieces out and steam gently without
allowing the iron to touch the yarn.
Join both shoulder seams using back stitch
or mattress stitch if preferred.

Neckband
With RS facing, using 2¾mm (US 2) needles
and yarn A, slip 13 (13: 13: 13: 13: 14) sts
from right front holder onto right needle,
rejoin yarn and pick up and knit 20 (24: 28:
30: 28: 32) sts up right side of neck,
35 (37: 37: 39: 39: 41) sts from back,
and 20 (24: 28: 30: 28: 32) sts down left
side of neck, then patt across 13 (13: 13:
13: 13: 14) sts on left front holder.
101 (111: 119: 125: 121: 133) sts.
Beg with a K row, work in rev st st for
4 rows, ending with a **RS** row.
Cast off knitwise (on **WS**).

Frills (make 6)
Cast on 280 (280: 288: 296: 296: 304) sts
using 3mm (US 2/3) needles and yarn **A**
DOUBLE.
Break off yarn **A** and join in yarn **B.**
(**Note**: Yarn is used single from this point on.)
Row 1 (RS): *sl 1, K1, psso, rep from
* to end.
140 (140: 144: 148: 148: 152) sts.
Row 2: Purl.
Row 3: As row 1.
70 (70: 72: 74: 74: 76) sts.
Rows 4 and 5: Knit.
Cast off knitwise (on **WS**).
Using photograph as a guide, sew cast-off
edges of frills along frill placement lines
on fronts.
Join side seams. Join sleeve seams.
Insert sleeves into armholes.
Sew on buttons.

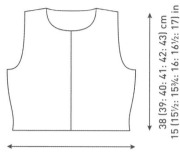

38 (39: 40: 41: 42: 43) cm
15 (15½: 15¾: 16: 16½: 17) in

40.5 (43: 45: 48.5: 51: 55) cm
16 (17: 18: 19: 20: 21½) in

45 (46: 47: 48: 49: 50) cm
17¾ (18: 18½: 19: 19¼: 19¾) in

INDIGO
CHICEST CABLED DUSTER COAT

Recommendation
Suitable for the knitter with a little experience
Please see pages 40 & 41 for photographs.

	XS	S	M	L	XL	XXL	
To fit	**81**	**86**	**91**	**97**	**102**	**109**	cm
bust	32	34	36	38	40	43	in

Rowan Big Wool
12 13 14 14 15 16 x 100gm
Photographed in Commodore

Needles
1 pair 9mm (no 00) (US 13) needles
1 pair 10mm (no 000) (US 15) needles
Cable needle

Buttons · 3

Tension
9 sts and 14 rows to 10 cm measured over
moss stitch using 10mm (US 15) needles.

SPECIAL ABBREVIATIONS
C6B = slip next 3 sts onto cable needle and
leave at back of work, K3, then K3 from cable
needle; **C6F** = slip next 3 sts onto cable
needle and leave at front of work, K3, then K3
from cable needle.

Pattern note: When casting off sts for
shoulders, slip the first st of the cast-off row
(rather than knitting or purling it) so that less
of a step is created along the entire shoulder
edge. At top of each cable, work (K2tog) 3
times (or (P2tog) 3 times) when casting off –
the number of sts given to be cast off to NOT
take into account these decreases.

BACK
Cast on 47 (49: 51: 53: 55: 59) sts using
10mm (US 15) needles.
Row 1 (RS): K1 (0: 1: 1: 0: 0), (P1, K1) 2
(3: 3: 3: 4: 5) times, *P1, (inc in next st, K1)
twice*, rep from * to * once more, (P1, K1)
8 (8: 8: 9: 9: 9) times, rep from * to * twice
more, P1, (K1, P1) 2 (3: 3: 3: 4: 5) times,
K1 (0: 1: 1: 0: 0).
55 (57: 59: 61: 63: 67) sts.
Row 2: K1 (0: 1: 1: 0: 0), (P1, K1) 2 (3: 3:
3: 4: 5) times, *K1, (P6, K1) twice*, place
marker on needle, K1, (P1, K1) 7 (7: 7: 8:
8: 8) times, place marker on needle,
rep from * to * once more, (K1, P1)
2 (3: 3: 3: 4: 5) times, K1 (0: 1: 1: 0: 0).
These 2 rows set the sts – 2 cable panels
with moss st between and at sides.
Keeping sts correct, cont in moss st
and cable patt as folls:
Row 1 (RS): Moss st 5 (6: 7: 7: 8: 10) sts,
P1, (K6, P1) twice, slip marker onto
right needle, moss st 15 (15: 15: 17:
17: 17) sts, slip marker onto right needle,
rep from * to * once more, moss st 5 (6: 7:
7: 8: 10) sts.
Row 2: Moss st 5 (6: 7: 7: 8: 10) sts,
K1, (P6, K1) twice, slip marker onto
right needle, moss st 15 (15: 15: 17:
17: 17) sts, slip marker onto right needle,
rep from * to * once more, moss st 5 (6: 7:
7: 8: 10) sts.
Rows 3 to 8: As rows 1 and 2, 3 times.
Row 9: Moss st 5 (6: 7: 7: 8: 10) sts, *P1,
C6B, P1, C6F, P1*, slip marker onto right
needle, M1, moss st 15 (15: 15: 17: 17: 17)
sts, M1, slip marker onto right needle, rep
from * to * once more, moss st 5 (6: 7: 7:
8: 10) sts.
57 (59: 61: 63: 65: 69) sts.
Row 10: Moss st 5 (6: 7: 7: 8: 10) sts,
K1, (P6, K1) twice, slip marker onto
right needle, moss st 17 (17: 17: 19:
19: 19) sts, slip marker onto right needle,
rep from * to * once more, moss st 5 (6: 7:
7: 8: 10) sts.
These 10 rows form moss st and cable patt
and beg shaping.
Work 18 (18: 20: 20: 20: 20) rows, inc
1 st at each end of 9th (9th: 11th: 11th:

11th: 11th) of these rows and ending
with a WS row.
59 (61: 63: 65: 67: 71) sts.
Next row (RS): Patt to marker, slip
marker onto right needle, M1, patt to
next marker, M1, slip marker onto right
needle, patt to end.
61 (63: 65: 67: 69: 73) sts.
Work 19 rows, inc 1 st at each end of 10th
of these rows and ending with a WS row.
63 (65: 67: 69: 71: 75) sts.
Next row (RS): Inc in first st, patt to marker,
slip marker onto right needle, M1, patt to
next marker, M1, slip marker onto right
needle, patt to last st, inc in last st.
67 (69: 71: 73: 75: 79) sts.
Inc 1 st at each end of 4th and foll 5 alt rows,
taking inc sts into moss st.
79 (81: 83: 85: 87: 91) sts.
Work 1 row, ending with a WS row.
Cast on 3 (3: 4: 5: 5: 5) sts at beg of
next 2 rows, then 3 (4: 4: 5: 6: 6) sts at
beg of foll 2 rows.
91 (95: 99: 105: 109: 113) sts.
Place markers at both ends of last row
to denote base of armhole opening.
Next row (RS): Patt to within 17 sts of
marker, work 2 tog, patt 15 sts, slip marker
onto right needle, M1, patt to next marker,
M1, slip marker onto right needle, patt 15 sts,
work 2 tog tbl, patt to end.
Work 19 rows.
Next row (RS): Patt to within 17 sts of
marker, work 2 tog, patt 15 sts, slip marker
onto right needle, M1, patt to next marker,
M1, slip marker onto right needle, patt 15 sts,
work 2 tog tbl, patt to end.
Cont straight until back measures 26 (27: 27:
28: 29: 30) cm **from markers**, ending with
a WS row.
Shape shoulders
Keeping patt correct and referring to pattern
note, cast off 4 (5: 5: 6: 6: 7) sts at beg of
next 2 (6: 2: 6: 2: 6) rows, then 5 (6: 6: 7: 7:
8) sts at beg of foll 6 (2: 6: 2: 6: 2) rows,
then 17 sts at beg of foll row, ending with
a **RS** row.
Cast off rem 36 (36: 36: 38: 38: 38) sts,
placing marker after first 17 cast-off sts
(to denote left side of back neck).

LEFT FRONT

Cast on 27 (28: 29: 30: 31: 33) sts using 10mm (US 15) needles.

Row 1 (RS): K1 (0: 1: 1: 0: 0), (P1, K1) 2 (3: 3: 3: 4: 5) times, *P1, (inc in next st, K1) twice*, rep from * to * once more, (P1, K1) 6 times, P0 (0: 0: 1: 1: 1).

31 (32: 33: 34: 35: 37) sts.

Row 2: K1 (1: 1: 0: 0: 0), (P1, K1) 5 (5: 5: 6: 6: 6) times, place marker on needle, K1, (P6, K1) twice, (K1, P1) 2 (3: 3: 3: 4: 5) times, K1 (0: 1: 1: 0: 0).

These 2 rows set the sts – cable panel with moss st at both sides.

Keeping sts correct, cont in moss st and cable patt as folls:

Row 1 (RS): Moss st 5 (6: 7: 7: 8: 10) sts, P1, (K6, P1) twice, slip marker onto right needle, moss st 11 (11: 11: 12: 12: 12) sts.

Row 2: Moss st 11 (11: 11: 12: 12: 12) sts, slip marker onto right needle, K1, (P6, K1) twice, moss st 5 (6: 7: 7: 8: 10) sts.

Rows 3 to 8: As rows 1 and 2, 3 times.

Row 9: Moss st 5 (6: 7: 7: 8: 10) sts, P1, C6B, P1, C6F, P1, slip marker onto right needle, M1, moss st 11 (11: 11: 12: 12: 12) sts.

32 (33: 34: 35: 36: 38) sts.

Row 10: Moss st 12 (12: 12: 13: 13: 13) sts, slip marker onto right needle, K1, (P6, K1) twice, moss st 5 (6: 7: 7: 8: 10) sts.

These 10 rows form moss st and cable patt and beg shaping.

Work 18 (18: 20: 20: 20: 20) rows, inc 1 st at beg of 9th (9th: 11th: 11th: 11th: 11th) of these rows and ending with a WS row.

33 (34: 35: 36: 37: 39) sts.

Next row (RS): Patt to marker, slip marker onto right needle, M1, patt to end.

34 (35: 36: 37: 38: 40) sts.

Work 19 rows, inc 1 st at beg of 10th of these rows and ending with a WS row.

35 (36: 37: 38: 39: 41) sts.

Next row (RS): Inc in first st, patt to marker, slip marker onto right needle, M1, patt to end.

37 (38: 39: 40: 41: 43) sts.

Inc 1 st at beg of 4th and foll 5 alt rows, taking inc sts into moss st.

43 (44: 45: 46: 47: 49) sts.

Work 1 row, ending with a WS row.

Cast on 3 (3: 4: 5: 5: 5) sts at beg of next row, then 3 (4: 4: 5: 6: 6) sts at beg of foll alt row.

49 (51: 53: 56: 58: 60) sts.

Work 1 row, ending with a WS row.

Place marker at end of last row to denote base of armhole opening.

Next row (RS): Patt to within 17 sts of marker, work 2 tog, patt 15 sts, slip marker onto right needle, M1, patt to end.

Work 19 rows.

Next row (RS): Patt to within 17 sts of marker, work 2 tog, patt 15 sts, slip marker onto right needle, M1, patt to end.

Cont straight until 3 rows less have been worked than on back to beg of shoulder shaping, ending with a **RS** row.

Shape neck

Keeping patt correct, cast off 7 (7: 7: 8: 8: 8) sts at beg of next row.

42 (44: 46: 48: 50: 52) sts.

Next row (RS): Patt to last 5 sts, work 3 tog tbl, patt 2 sts. 40 (42: 44: 46: 48: 50) sts.

Working all neck decreases as set by last row, cont as folls:

Work 1 row, ending with a WS row.

Shape shoulder

Keeping patt correct and referring to pattern note, cast off 4 (5: 5: 6: 6: 7) sts at beg of next and foll 0 (2: 0: 2: 0: 2) alt rows, then 5 (6: 6: 7: 7: 8) sts at beg of foll 3 (1: 3: 1: 3: 1) alt rows **and at same time** dec 2 sts at neck edge of next and foll alt row. 17 sts.

Work 1 row, ending with a WS row.

Cast off rem 17 sts.

RIGHT FRONT

Cast on 27 (28: 29: 30: 31: 33) sts using 10mm (US 15) needles.

Row 1 (RS): P0 (0: 0: 1: 1: 1), (K1, P1) 6 times, *(inc in next st, K1) twice, P1*, rep from * to * once more, (K1, P1) 2 (3: 3: 3: 4: 5) times, K1 (0: 1: 1: 0: 0).

31 (32: 33: 34: 35: 37) sts.

Row 2: K1 (0: 1: 1: 0: 0), (P1, K1) 2 (3: 3: 3: 4: 5) times, K1, (P6, K1) twice, place marker on needle, (K1, P1) 5 (5: 5: 6: 6: 6) times, K1 (1: 1: 0: 0: 0),

These 2 rows set the sts – cable panel with moss st at both sides.

Keeping sts correct, cont in moss st and cable patt as folls:

Row 1 (RS): Moss st 11 (11: 11: 12: 12: 12) sts, slip marker onto right needle, P1, (K6, P1) twice, moss st 5 (6: 7: 7: 8: 10) sts.

Row 2: Moss st 5 (6: 7: 7: 8: 10) sts, K1, (P6, K1) twice, slip marker onto right needle, moss st 11 (11: 11: 12: 12: 12) sts.

Rows 3 to 8: As rows 1 and 2, 3 times.

Row 9: Moss st 11 (11: 11: 12: 12: 12) sts, M1, slip marker onto right needle, P1, C6B, P1, C6F, P1, moss st 5 (6: 7: 7: 8: 10) sts.

32 (33: 34: 35: 36: 38) sts.

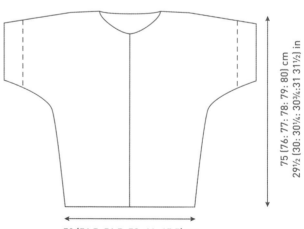

75 [76: 77: 78: 79: 80] cm
29½ [30: 30¼: 30¾: 31: 31½] in

52 (54.5: 56.5: 59: 61: 65.5) cm
20½ (21½: 22½: 23½: 24: 26) in

Row 10: Moss st 5 (6: 7: 7: 8: 10) sts, K1, (P6, K1) twice, slip marker onto right needle, moss st 12 (12: 12: 13: 13: 13) sts.
These 10 rows form moss st and cable patt and beg shaping.
Work 18 (18: 20: 20: 20: 20) rows, inc 1 st at end of 9th (9th: 11th: 11th: 11th: 11th) of these rows and ending with a WS row.
33 (34: 35: 36: 37: 39) sts.
Next row (RS): Patt to marker, M1, slip marker onto right needle, patt to end.
34 (35: 36: 37: 38: 40) sts.
Work 19 rows, inc 1 st at end of 10th of these rows and ending with a WS row.
35 (36: 37: 38: 39: 41) sts.
Next row (RS): Patt to marker, M1, slip marker onto right needle, patt to last st, inc in last st. 37 (38: 39: 40: 41: 43) sts.
Inc 1 st at end of 4th and foll 4 alt rows, taking inc sts into moss st.
42 (43: 44: 45: 46: 48) sts.
Work 1 row, ending with a WS row.

Next row (buttonhole row) (RS): Patt 2 sts, work 2 tog tbl, (yrn) twice, work 2 tog (to make a buttonhole – on next row work twice tbl into the double yrn), patt to last st, inc in last st. 43 (44: 45: 46: 47: 49) sts.
Working a further 2 buttonholes in this way on 16th (16th: 16th: 18th: 18th: 18th) and foll 16th (16th: 16th: 18th: 18th: 18th) row, complete to match left front, reversing shapings.

MAKING UP
Pin the pieces out and steam gently without allowing the iron to touch the yarn.
Join both shoulder seams using back stitch or mattress stitch if preferred.

Neck edging
With RS facing and using 9mm (US 13) needles, beg and ending at front opening edges, pick up and knit 19 (19: 19: 20: 20: 20) sts up right side of neck, 21 (21: 21: 23: 23: 23) sts from back, then 19 (19: 19: 20: 20: 20) sts down left side of neck. 59 (59: 59: 63: 63: 63) sts.
Cast off knitwise (on **WS**).

Cuffs (both alike)
With RS facing and using 9mm (US 13) needles, pick up and knit 54 (56: 56: 58: 60: 62) sts evenly along row-end edge between markers.
Row 1 (WS): P0 (1: 1: 0: 1: 0), *K2, P2, rep from * to last 2 (3: 3: 2: 3: 2) sts, K2, P0 (1: 1: 0: 1: 0).
Row 2: K0 (1: 1: 0: 1: 0), *P2, K2, rep from * to last 2 (3: 3: 2: 3: 2) sts, P2, K0 (1: 1: 0: 1: 0).
These 2 rows form rib.
Cont in rib for a further 17 rows, ending with a WS row.
Cast off in rib.
Join side and cuff seams, reversing cuff seams for last 12 rows. Fold cuff to RS as in photograph and secure to overarm and underarm seams. Sew on buttons.

INFORMATION

TENSION

Achieving the correct tension has to be one of the most important elements in producing a beautiful, well fitting knitted garment. The tension controls the size and shape of your finished piece and any variation to either stitches or rows, however slight, will affect your work and change the fit completely.

To avoid any disappointment, we would always recommend that you knit a tension square in the yarn and stitch given in the pattern, working perhaps four or five more stitches and rows than those given in the tension note.

When counting the tension, place your knitting on a flat surface and mark out a 10cm square with pins. Count the stitches between the pins. If you have too many stitches to 10cm your knitting it too tight, try again using thicker needles, if you have too few stitches to 10cm your knitting is too loose, so try again using finer needles. Please note, if you are unable to achieve the correct stitches and rows required, the stitches are more crucial as many patterns are knitted to length.

Keep an eye on your tension during knitting, especially if you're going back to work which has been put to one side for any length of time.

SIZING

The instructions are given for the smallest size. Where they vary, work the figures in brackets for the larger sizes. One set of figures refers to all sizes. The size diagram with each pattern will help you decide which size to knit. The measurements given on the size diagram are the actual size your garment should be when completed. Measurements will vary from design to design because the necessary ease allowances have been made in each pattern to give your garment the correct fit, i.e. a loose fitting garment will be several cm wider than a neat fitted one, a snug fitting garment may have no ease at all.

WRAP STITCH

A wrap stitch is used to eliminate the hole created when using the short row shaping method. Work to the position on the row indicated in the pattern, wrap the next st (by slipping next st onto right needle, taking yarn to opposite side of work between needles and then slipping same st back onto left needle – on foll rows, K tog the loop and the wrapped st) and turn, cont from pattern.

BEADING

Bead 1 (RS rows) = place a bead by bringing yarn to front (RS) of work and slipping bead up next to st just worked, slip next st purlwise from left needle to right needle and return yarn to back (WS) of work, leaving bead sitting in front of slipped st on RS. Do not place beads on edge sts of rows as this will interfere with seaming and picking up sts.

Beading note

Before starting to knit, thread beads onto yarn. To do this, thread a fine sewing needle (one which will easily pass through the beads) with sewing thread. Knot ends of thread and then pass end of yarn through this loop. Thread a bead onto sewing thread and then gently slide it along and onto knitting yarn. Continue in this way until required numbers of beads are on yarn.

WORKING A LACE PATTERN

When working a lace pattern it is important to remember that if you are unable to work a full repeat i.e. both the increase and corresponding decrease and vice versa, the stitches should be worked in stocking stitch or an alternative stitch suggested in the pattern.

CHART NOTE

Some of our patterns include a chart. Each square on a chart represent a stitch and each line of squares a row of knitting.

When working from a chart, unless otherwise stated, read odd rows (RS) from right to left and even rows (WS) from left to right. The key alongside each chart indicates how each stitch is worked.

FINISHING INSTRUCTIONS

It is the pressing and finishing which will transform your knitted pieces into a garment to be proud of.

Pressing

Darn in ends neatly along the selvage edge. Follow closely any special instructions given on the pattern or ball band and always take great care not to over press your work.

Block out your knitting on a pressing or ironing board, easing into shape, and unless otherwise states, press each piece using a warm iron over a damp cloth.

Tip: Attention should be given to ribs/edgings; if the garment is close fitting – steam the ribs gently so that the stitches fill out but stay elastic.

Alternatively if the garment is to hang straight then steam out to the correct shape.

Tip: Take special care to press the selvages, as this will make sewing up both easier and neater.

CONSTRUCTION
Stitching together

When stitching the pieces together, remember to match areas of pattern very carefully where they meet. Use a stitch such as back stitch or mattress stitch for all main knitting seams and join all ribs and neckband with mattress stitch, unless otherwise stated.

Take extra care when stitching the edgings and collars around the back neck of a garment. They control the width of the back neck, and if too wide the garment will be ill fitting and drop off the shoulder. Knit back neck edgings only to the length stated in the pattern, even stretching it slightly if for example, you are working in garter or horizontal rib stitch.

Stitch edgings/collars firmly into place using a back stitch seam, easing-in the back neck to fit the collar/edging rather than stretching the collar/edging to fit the back neck.

Straight cast-off sleeves: Place centre of cast-off edge of sleeve to shoulder seams. Sew top of sleeve to body, using markers as guidelines where applicable. Join side and sleeve seams.

Set-in sleeves: Join side and sleeve seams. Place centre of cast off edge of sleeve to shoulder seams. Set in sleeve, easing sleeve head into armhole.

CARE INSTRUCTIONS
Yarns
Follow the care instructions printed on each individual ball band. Where different yarns are used in the same garment, follow the care instructions for the more delicate one.

Buttons
We recommend that buttons are removed if your garment is to be machine washed.

ABBREVIATIONS

K	knit
P	purl
K1b	knit 1 through back loop
st(s)	stitch(es)
inc	increas(e)(ing)
dec	decreas(e)(ing)
st st	stocking stitch (1 row K, 1 row P)
garter st	garter stitch (K every row)
beg	begin(ning)
foll	following
rem	remain(ing)
rev st st	reverse stocking stitch (1 row P, 1 row K)
rep	repeat
alt	alternate
cont	continue
patt	pattern
tog	together
mm	millimetres
cm	centimetres
in(s)	inch(es)
RS	right side
WS	wrong side
sl 1	slip one stitch
psso	pass slipped stitch over
tbl	through back of loop
M1	make one stitch by picking up horizontal loop before next stitch and knitting into back of it
M1p	make one stitch by picking up horizontal loop before next stitch and purling into back of it
yfwd	yarn forward
yon	yarn over needle
yrn	yarn round needle
Mp	Make picot: Cast on 1 st, by inserting the right needle between the first and second stitch on left needle, take yarn round needle, bring loop through and place on left (one stitch cast on), cast off 1 st, by knitting first the loop and then the next stitch, pass the first stitch over the second (one stitch cast off).
Cn	cabl needle
C4B	Cable 4 back: Slip next 2 sts onto a cn and hold at back of work, K2, K2 from cn.
C4F	Cable 4 front: Slip next 2 sts onto a cn and hold at front of work, K2, K2 from cn.

THANK YOU'S

Sincere thanks Jill & John for welcoming us into your wonderful home. Holme Castle without doubt provided the most perfect setting for the beautiful photographs, we truly appreciated your warmth & hospitality & for not flinching at the havoc that ensued whilst we were shooting.

As always we have many others to thank including our amazing team, Graham & Angela, Diana, Fiona, Hannah, Rebecca, Angharad & Jackie, Sue, Tricia, Susan, Ella, Sandra, Betty, Arna, Glennis & Mary.

Also, Howard & Jen, Tony & Joan, Lindsay, Ann, Simon, Helene at Revival Vintage, Rachel at Briggs & Oliver Antiques, and last but by no means least, David & Rufus.

We couldn't have produced this book without each & every one of you!

Holme Castle offers guest accommodation
& Felt making tuition.
Email: jillhayfield@live.co.uk
Tel: 01484 680680
Mobile: 0775 38 39 222

Revival – www.revivalvintage.co.uk
Briggs & Oliver – www.briggsandoliver.co.uk

INDEX